More than Symbol

MORE THAN SYMBOL

Eli Landrum, Jr.

BROADMAN PRESS
Nashville, Tennessee

© Copyright 1983 ● Broadman Press

All rights reserved. 4223-04

ISBN: 0-8054-2304-4

Dewey Decimal Classification: 264.36

Subject Heading: LORD'S SUPPER

Library of Congress Catalog Card Number: 81-86669

Printed in the United States of America

To my dad
and to the memory of my mother
To Odell and Wenona Grice,
the world's greatest in-laws

Contents

Introduction

In July 1965, I began a pastoral internship at the Dauphin Way Baptist Church in Mobile, Alabama. I was an intern assistant to the pastor, Dr. Harold W. Seever. I was to work under Dr. Seever's leadership for less than a year; he retired in March of 1966 and died in September of the same year. During the months that I was associated with him, I learned a great deal from him— by direct instruction and by observation.

One thing that impressed me was Dr. Seever's careful attention to the Lord's Supper celebration. He reinforced my conviction that the supper should be the center of a worship period, not tacked on to the end almost as a footnote or an afterthought. He always had a meditation or short sermon that highlighted some facet of the Master's meal. And he emphasized every detail so that the celebration ran smoothly. Nothing was left to chance or guesswork; nobody involved in serving the supper "played it by ear." Everyone knew exactly what to do, how to do it, and when to do it.

Because of this training, I determined to lead such periods of worship in such a way as to make the meal as meaningful as possible. From that determination came the thirty meditations that follow. They are brief, but they seek to draw out some of the dramatic, suggestive implications of the supper. You will discover quickly that I have drawn on the written wisdom of a number of incisive people, especially George A. Buttrick and Halford E. Luccock. I make no claim to be original. I merely have tried to put the Lord's Supper in the lofty place that I feel it should have in our worship.

1

More than Symbol

1 Corinthians 11:23-28

In 1 Corinthians 11:23-28, we have Paul's account of the institution of the Lord's Supper. This was what he "received of the Lord," he wrote. Probably, this was the tradition that he had received from members of the early church. In Paul's conversation with the disciples who were present when Jesus instituted his meal, Paul learned the details of the Savior's Supper. This is the earliest written account we have of the Lord's Supper's beginning. It is important because it gives us valuable insight into this meal's meaning and significance to the early church.

Paul wrote 1 Corinthians 11:23-28 in an attempt to correct a serious problem in the church at Corinth. In verses 20-21, he indicated that the Christians at Corinth had distorted and abused the supper; they had lost a true sense of its purpose, message, and creative meaning. Some were bringing their own food and eating it without sharing with others who had little—or without waiting for others to arrive. Therefore, some were filled while others were hungry. In addition, some drank a great deal of wine, causing them to become intoxicated. Thus, the Lord's Supper was a meaningless event in the church, a source of difficulty, and an occasion of mockery by those who viewed it from the outside. Paul wrote in order to set the Corinthian Christians straight concerning their participation in the supper. In so doing, he gave us his feelings about one of the two ordinances which Christ left for his church to experience.

We, too, need to have a wholesome view of the Lord's Supper. We must have a clear understanding of its significance

11

and deep meaning. We do not come to gorge ourselves, but to receive a small piece of unleavened bread. Neither do we become intoxicated, but we drink a tiny glass of grape juice. Even so, if we are not careful, we do violence to this meal in other ways. *We are prone to treat the supper as mere symbol or simply an acted parable, when in reality it is far more than either.* The Lord's table, the bread, and the cup are symbols; if they are employed correctly, they point beyond themselves and become part of something immeasureably meaningful to the participants. What we do is more than custom or habit. It is more than a set time on a church calendar. And in what we do, we seek to make proper use of suggestive symbols.

Symbols have legitimate places in our living. For instance, our nation's flag is a well-known symbol. It is nothing more than a piece of cloth with stars and varicolored stripes on it. And sometimes, when we see it displayed, that is all it is to us; in fact, we may be only vaguely aware of its presence. But at times, we see it and begin to remember what it stands for. It stands for people who wanted freedom to govern themselves and were willing to pay the price for it. Countless individuals gave themselves in defense of their country, its ideals, its people; and committed themselves to a continuing experiment in personal freedom under God. And we are led into an experience which can be deeply moving, an experience of sincere gratitude, great pride, and renewed determination that we will be one nation under God, trying to fulfill his purpose for us.

The cross is a symbol. Today, it is constructed of wood, stone, or metal and serves as a reminder of an ancient method of putting criminals to death. It is displayed on church steeples, in the front of church auditoriums, and in cemeteries. Small gold or silver crosses on chains are worn as jewelry. The cross is a common sight whose meaning may not even register with those who view it. But to those who stop and reflect, the cross symbolizes God's grace to undeserving people. It moves them to expressions of worship in which gratitude and petitions for forgiveness are integral parts.

Symbols can be employed legitimately in worship, as long as they are looked on as instruments of worship—reminders, helps, inducements to reverence. Symbols can be useful, meaningful, and significant if they point beyond themselves to a genuine, creative experience.

The table, the bread, and the cup are symbols. In themselves, they are not sacred. But the experience of which they are a part is sacred, a holy moment in our Christian lives. The experience in which we share as partakers of the Master's meal goes far beyond symbol.

Sharing in the Lord's Supper is an experience in which we enjoy a deliberate stillness, a quiet time of deep reverence in which we acknowledge God's sovereignty over all of life—and over our individual lives. It is a brief period in which we shut out the noise and rush of our living to open life to God in worship. Among fellow believers, we ask from God and offer ourselves to God anew.

In reflecting on these symbols and the symbolic meaning that Christ attached to them, we are stirred again with a new realization of how much God has done for us, how deeply he has loved us, and how unfailingly he continues to love us. We live in a love that gave supremely and goes on giving.

In partaking of the symbolic elements in the Lord's Supper, we profess our participation in Christ's body, the church. We confess our continuing need of him and the inner strength that he gives. And we commit ourselves again to his use in his high purpose.

So, the unique symbols of the Master's meal become part of a larger, deeper experience of creative worship—worship in which we experience fellowship with the present Christ and with his people. What we do in the supper is much more than symbol;[1] it is vitalizing spiritual refreshing, a restocking of the deep wells of our living.

NOTE
1. I owe this idea to Dr. Frank Stagg, who used the phrase and pursued the concept in a graduate seminar at New Orleans Baptist Theological Seminary.

2

Affirmation of Presence

John 14:18,28

Each year we gather on Easter—more of us than usual—to celebrate Jesus' resurrection from the dead. We sing and say, "He lives!" in gratitude and praise. More often during the year, we come to moments of a celebration not quite as large and attractive as Easter. We come to share an experience in whose quietness and simplicity we acknowledge a continuing Presence with us.

In the Gospel of John, we discover two striking statements which hit at the central thrust of the Lord's Supper. John did not record the institution of the Master's meal as did the other three Gospel writers and Paul. John did describe a final meal that Jesus shared with his disciples near Passover. In this context, John preserved the scene of Jesus washing his men's feet. Jesus talked of his approaching betrayal and appealed once more to Judas. Jesus gave his new command to love and predicted Peter's denial. A long dialogue with his disciples followed which closed with what is called Jesus' high priestly prayer. In the context of a meal, included in lengthy discourse, Jesus said something remarkable and repeated it: "I will not leave you comfortless: I will come to you." "Ye have heard how I said unto you, I go away, and come again unto you." Our participation in the Lord's Supper is our affirmation that that promise is fulfilled in our lives. We celebrate the reality of his presence with us—here and in other moments and places of our living.

I like what George Buttrick wrote about the symbols of the Christian faith. He noted: "The symbol of the Christian faith is not an hourglass or a grave, but an empty cross and an empty grave—and bread from living seed, with wine from living vines. Perhaps we should say that Christianity has no fixed or absolute symbols: it has a Presence."[1]

Why do we, as a church, participate in the Lord's Supper on a regular schedule? Do we do so solely as an act of obedience to Jesus' command that we keep it as a memorial? Is our regular participation due to the fact that this is a church practice of long standing? Do we meet merely to review facts of redemptive history? Or do we meet to acknowledge the presence of One who makes a creative difference, all the difference, in life? Unless we come to confirm that Jesus' words in Matthew 28:20, "Lo, I am with you alway, even unto the end of the world," are expressive of our present experience, we miss the meaning of the meal.

What Frank Stagg has suggested concerning the Lord's Supper appeals to me: The experience of the supper views Calvary from the distance of years. We look back to a cross on a hill.[2] To my mind, such a backward look can be legitimate and productive. We never waste time when we look seriously at what transpired on Golgotha many years ago. There, as Paul expressed it in Romans 5:8, God was proving his love for us "in that, while we were yet sinners, Christ died for us." We see again life given in love to redeem the unlovely; we view God in Christ reconciling lost humanity to himself. We hear God appealing to the highest in people, offering forgiveness, offering life, and calling persons into the narrow way. And we celebrate the fact that the crucified Carpenter left a tomb to rejoin his people, no longer limited by the physical. He is the Risen Crucified, present in power.

The Lord's Supper looks ahead to the returning Lord. One of the earliest and most consistent affirmations of the Christian faith is that the Christ who was crucified, who was raised, and who ascended will come again. He will appear in climactic triumph to close the book on history. He will come in finality, to be recognized by the willing, and the unwilling as well, as Lord. In a meantime of whatever length, he is present to continue his redemptive work among people.

He was crucified—but he lives! He will come again—but he is here! So we come to celebrate Presence, to open life to him in a deliberate act of worship, to ask his continuing presence and activity in our daily living.

By our participation in Christ's meal, we affirm that he is present *in his church.* We recognize that the church incarnates our Lord in our world. We confess that we are more than a body of people; we are the body of Christ. He continues to love, serve, and appeal to people through his church.

We come to acknowledge that Christ is present *in our individual lives*—to say that Paul's words in Colossians 1:27 were not empty musing: "Christ in you, the hope of glory." We come to make Paul's words in Galatians 2:20 our own: "I am crucified with Christ: nevertheless I live; yet not I, but Christ liveth in me." We come to affirm his presence because we encounter him daily.

The risen, living Christ is present to support in efforts made in his Spirit and in the common experiences that life presents. He is present to challenge the best in us to quality living, service, and leadership; to lead toward maturity, toward more complete equipping for life; to share the variety of our living. He comes to us to teach us, to throw more light on his approach to living. He is present to inspire, to encourage, to urge us on in our pilgrimages. He is with us in transforming friendship.

We meet in worship to affirm Presence. We serve a living Savior.

NOTES
1. George A. Buttrick, *The Interpreter's Bible* (Nashville: Abingdon Press, 1951), 7:576.
2. Frank Stagg, *New Testament Theology* (Nashville: Broadman Press, 1962), p. 247.

3

Celebration of Deliverance

I Corinthians 11:23-28; Mark 14:22-25

Jesus chose the time of the Jewish Passover to institute his own meal for his church. One cannot avoid the strong feeling that he did so for an express purpose.

The Jews observed the Passover feast in order to celebrate one of the most significant events, if not *the* most important event, in their history. The celebration goes back to a time in the Hebrews' early experience in which God's purpose and power were revealed in unmistakable fashion. The Hebrews writhed under the Egyptians' oppressive heels. God selected Moses as his spokesman and sent him to Egypt's ruler with the demand that the Hebrews be released. The Egyptian ruler refused, and a series of events followed in which God worked to gain freedom for his people. But the pharaoh remained obstinate and maintained his determination to hold the Hebrews as slaves.

Finally, the Hebrews were told to prepare for a monumental event. The death angel was going to pass over the land, and the firstborn in every family would be killed. If each Hebrew family would kill a lamb and sprinkle the blood on the two side posts and on the upper doorpost of the house, that family would be spared the anguish of losing the firstborn. The Hebrews did as they were told; and, at the appointed time, it happened as God had said. Widespread death of the oldest children in Egyptian families occurred. Pharaoh hastily called for Moses and Aaron— the Bible says by night—and told them to get the Hebrews and leave. Likewise, the Egyptian people were so anxious to be rid of the Hebrews that they helped the captive people to leave. And

18

so, the Israelites were delivered from Egypt.

In Exodus 12:24, Moses instructed the Hebrews: "Ye shall observe this thing for an ordinance to thee and to thy sons for ever." Each year the Jews gathered to observe the Passover; they met to eat the same meal and to observe the various rules for the same number of days as had their forefathers. These Jews, thus, participated in a constant reminder of God's marvelous working on their behalf. They looked on the Passover and the Exodus from Egypt as the concrete, historical evidence that God had chosen them to be his people in a unique sense. As each generation kept the Passover, the people celebrated a deliverance which God had worked.

In the Passover context, Jesus instituted his meal. *And he meant for it to be a celebration of the deliverance he was effecting for people.* By what he did at the first meal, he expressed what he was about to do for all people who would respond to him. He was going to make possible a spiritual exodus greater and more significant than the Exodus from Egypt in the Jews' history. We who meet to participate in Christ's meal have participated in the deliverance Christ made possible. We know that, as 1 John 3:14 states, we have "passed from death unto life." Christ meant to make possible for us an exodus. In Luke 9:31, in the account of the transfiguration, Luke recorded that the disciples saw Jesus speaking with Moses and Elijah; they were talking about "his decease which he should accomplish at Jerusalem." The word *decease* in Greek literally is *exodus.* By his dying, Jesus was going to work deliverance on a far deeper level than rescue from physical enslavement.

Because he gave his life, Christ has made available a deliverance from the oppressive bondage of sin. He has opened a way of escape from spiritual enslavement. Now we can advance toward full life in him. In the historical event of the cross and resurrection, an event which has no rival in the world's recorded history, God has shown that we are the subjects of his mercy. We know beyond doubt that God desires humanity to know the release which he can give. We could ask for no greater evidence that he desires for us to be his elect, chosen people.

In a sense, Jesus gave his followers a way to keep this redemptive event a fresh and living reality. The meal does not, and cannot, transport us back to the event itself; but it does place us in a context in which we are confronted once again with God's work of providing salvation.

The church—Christ's body—must participate in Christ's meal with a reverent sense of celebration. Someone has said that a Christian's whole life is a celebration of what God has done for that life. Our celebration of God's grace is focused in the Lord's Supper. In prayer, we express our deep awareness of and joy concerning the new life that God has given to us. We express our sincere gratitude for his deliverance. We pledge our continuing faithfulness and love.

We participate in the affairs of our world as people emancipated from ruin. Because of our deliverance, Peter declared in 1 Peter 2:9 that we are a "chosen generation, a royal priesthood, an holy nation, a peculiar people," that we "should shew forth the praises of him who hath called [us] out of darkness into his marvellous light." We, too, are people called out of bondage, made into a redemptive community, and given a commission.

And so we go on our way, celebrating quietly and constantly the deliverance that we enjoy and seeking to include others in this freedom. For we know that God has delivered us from meaninglessness, purposelessness. He has brought us out of stifling tyranny into his freedom. He wants to do this for every person. And *we* want this for *every* individual.

4

Pausing to Remember

1 Corinthians 11:23-26

One need we have in common, as the people of Christ, is a need to be reminded. The flow of information, events, people, and things can cause us to forget even some important items. Sometimes, things fail to register in their fullness; the force, vividness, and crucial meaning of events suffer time's wearing effects. We become careless with our storehouse of memories. *We need specific times of remembering.* For, as someone has noted, to remember is to make vivid, to make real, to make contemporary the effect of a deed.

If we utilize memory correctly, it is one of our greatest assets. By means of memory, we can bring warmth to cold days. We can gain light for our darkness, courage for our stern challenges, and inspiration for our drabness. Most of all, memory can restore lost incentive and purpose.

One thrust of the Lord's Supper is that it reminds us periodically of that which is central in our lives as Christ's followers. And we need to be reminded—by a dramatic act in which we participate as a fellowship. We participate in a shared act which impresses on us repeatedly that which we cannot allow to grow dim, faded, or worn—that which we cannot allow to be pushed off to one side in our lives.

Some have said that Paul made explicit in 1 Corinthians 11 what Jesus only implied in the original act in which he gave the supper to his church. And these go on to contend that the words, "This do in remembrance of me," have been added to Luke's account. Maybe so. But even if so, we have been done a tremendous service. For the Lord's Supper is an ever-timely reminder, imperative and crucial in the church's life. The supper is far more than this, but it is this: needed reminder.

We do not come to the Lord's table at the beginning of each quarter in the church year, a set number of times a year, or even every Sunday in the attempt to keep alive the memory of a man long dead and in danger of being forgotten. He is present among his people, and our action is not a matter of reviving a fading mental picture of Jesus. In reality, we celebrate his presence and power in his church.

We come to the Lord's table to call to mind again what God in Christ has done for us. We come to impress on our minds again what we have received. And we gather to respond to the Lord of the supper.

In the busy, bustling city around the little group in the upper room that night, all the memories of the Passover were being revived, as they were every year. According to Jewish literature, in the Passover celebration the son asks his father: "Why is this night different from other nights?" And the father responds by telling the story spanning the centuries. The story begins with a description of cruel slavery in Egypt, of a people deprived of their freedom. The account continues by narrating God's raising up a man to lead his people out of servitude to a liberty in which they could realize their destiny. The story ends on the high note of a nation's redemption. Jewish literature contains the idea that in every generation the people must view themselves as if they came out of Egypt themselves.

The night in which the Exodus began never was allowed to fade in the Jewish people's memories. The prophets repeatedly pointed the people to it. The psalmists sang of it. The people singled out this event and reexamined it, seeing again the many facets of its beauty. They reviewed its implications for their nation in every century and in every year. And every year they reenacted, recreated, this event.

Christians through the centuries have come together to share in the Lord's Supper. This sharing is not to remind themselves that Jesus of Nazareth once existed, but that the One present with them has done something on their behalf so creative that no amount of examination can reveal its fullness. We come to look again at what has been done for us, to find ever-new meaning in an old story.

We come to the Lord's table to be reminded of *Jesus' birth*. Its central meaning is for every day and not just for Christmas: God came to us as the God-man to share our living and to show a love that can free us to be his persons. God accepted willingly our limitations for a time in order to offer us limitless life.

We come to the supper to be reminded of *Christ's life*. His was the one solitary life the like of which had not been seen before and will not be seen again. His life had all the qualities every human being was intended to have—and we do not have. We are reminded of a unique life which summons us to higher levels of living. God redeems us in Christ.

And we come to be reminded of *the resurrection*. It has become the central fact of the church's life, a resurrection which forever speaks of life, of victory, and of a future. We come to have emphasized for us again God's sovereignty in his world.

We do well to pause and to remember. For when we do so, we can begin again with new inspiration and new determination. We can start out again with a sense of gratitude, deep indebtedness to God, and joy. And we experience a new beginning with the One who made possible the memories interwoven in the supper.

5

The New Covenant

1 Corinthians 11:23-28

Of highest significance in the context of Jesus' approaching suffering and death is that he spoke of a covenant based on what he was accomplishing. Paul called this the "new testament"— literally, the new covenant—with the clear implication that it was to replace the old covenant with Israel. This was the covenant which would supersede anything that had gone before.

Spoken in the context of his supper, Jesus' words concerning the new covenant would be understood readily by his disciples and by those who later heard and read his words. The idea of a covenant between God and people had played an important role in Israel's history. The Hebrews believed that God had made covenants with Abraham and the other patriarchs. They maintained that God had entered into a covenant relationship with Israel after he had delivered the nation from slavery in Egypt. The covenant's basis was God's mercy shown in his promise concerning what he would do for and through them if the Hebrews were obedient and faithful and if they discharged their responsibility.

We must understand what a covenant between God and persons is in the biblical record. It is not a mutual arrangement in which God and people come together and agree on terms. People do not assist in drawing up the conditions of their covenant relationship to God; they do not help to set up their own guidelines. God states the conditions, sets the standards, and outlines the requirements. God declares what he will do and what he expects from people. And persons are free to decide. They can accept the terms, which are always gracious and merciful, and enter a dynamic personal relationship to God. Or, they can refuse God's terms and exclude themselves from his covenant people. *This covenant relationship never is a matter of bargaining for terms; it is a matter of placing oneself under God's sovereign rule.*

The person who takes this step trusts that the God who draws up the covenant will keep his word; then the individual finds that what God gives in this covenant relationship is far more than one has a right to expect. If one adheres to the terms of God's covenant, God is able to lead that person to life in its highest fulfillment and meaning. If the covenant is refused or broken, then adverse results follow. But again, the emphasis must be made clear: people are free to accept or refuse; they are not free to modify God's covenant.

The most astonishing fact in this idea of covenant relationship to God often eludes us. We fail to grasp the amazing truth that although it is illogical that God who is holy would make a covenant with unholy persons, this is precisely what takes place. God who is righteous relates himself to people who can make no claim to righteousness. God who is gracious relates himself to people who often are prone to be ungracious. God who is merciful relates himself to individuals who frequently neither will receive nor give mercy. God's willingness to receive us ought to draw from us quiet and sincere gratitude. His willingness to relate himself personally to us is shown in the Lord's Supper, just as it was manifested in his dealings with the Hebrews.

The Hebrews were proud that they were the covenant people, but they came to the point where they wanted the blessings of such a relationship on their own terms, without meeting God's demands. The covenant was reduced to no more than an external keeping of the law instead of an internal change and a personal relationship to God.

The prophet Jeremiah saw the prevailing conditions of his day and spoke God's message concerning a new covenant to displace the old one. In Jeremiah 31:31-34, the prophet wrote of a new covenant of personal relationship and basic change rather than shallow, dead performance of duty. This new covenant would be based on God's forgiveness and love.

Paul may have had Jeremiah's words in mind when he wrote of the new covenant in 1 Corinthians 11:25. Beyond reasonable doubt, Jesus had the prophet's words in mind when he alluded to the covenant based on his life given for people (Mark 14:24). Jesus boldly declared that his covenant was based on his own self-giving; the underlying basis of his covenant was love and grace which worked recreation at the center of life. Because of this, the author of Hebrews wrote that Christ is the mediator of a better covenant established on better promises (Heb. 8:6)

As the disciples drank from the cup at the Last Supper, they were made aware by Jesus' words that they were participants in the new covenant relationship and that they were beneficiaries of God's work on their behalf. They were the new, reconstituted Israel living under God's rule and engaged in his ministry to people. They were now Christ's covenant people. The disciples were to live in a covenant relationship to Christ and to accept his requirements of faith, which acts, and love, which is received and shared.

As we come to participate in the Lord's Supper, and as we partake of the cup, we acknowledge our willingness to be Christ's covenant people. We give evidence that we have accepted his gracious and demanding terms for life; we show that we have assumed our privilege and our responsibility as his people. We express our awareness that we are participants in the new covenant because Christ gave himself for us and because we have allowed his self-giving to become operative in us.

As we share this experience, we renew our commitment to our Lord as his covenant people—stamped with his character, led by his presence, living in his grace. We come to the Lord's table—as his covenant people.

6

The Message of the Supper

1 Corinthians 11:23-29

Jesus had looked forward to observing the Passover with his disciples. He had made careful preparation. He had secured a private, upper room so that he could be alone with those nearest to him. Mark recorded that Jesus had given to two of his disciples the responsibility of preparing the Passover meal. Jesus had something to say to his men, in word and in act, which they needed to hear, see, and etch into their minds. At this point, they made up his church; that they understood him as far as they were able was vitally important. For he was about to go away, and they could not follow just yet. They would be without his physical presence to guide, instruct, encourage, and correct. He had shown and told them many things; that they retain at least the major thrust of his life and his death was crucial.

After the Passover meal, Jesus took some of the ingredients that were available and made of them a new meal with a new message. He gave to these ingredients fresh symbolism; they were to be used in a deep experience of renewal in the disciples' relationship to him.

Jesus chose bread to symbolize his body which would be given voluntarily for the disciples and for all peole who would respond to him. Bread was and is a mainstay, a necessity, the staff of life. It is a basic food for the body's nourishment. Jesus had used this item of food previously in his ministry to share a spiritual lesson with those who had gathered to hear him teach.

Perhaps the disciples remembered the miracle in which bread was involved. The day had been long and tiring. The

crowd that had formed to listen to Jesus had not taken time to
eat. Toward the end of the day, the fact that something would
have to be done became apparent. The people were hungry and
had made no provision. Someone discovered that, in the crowd,
one lad had a small lunch consisting of bread and fish. Jesus used
the small lunch to feed the crowd. He had intended to use this act
as the basis of a sermon, but the people were so awed, elated,
and stirred by the miracle that they gave no immediate opportunity for a sermon. They wanted Jesus for their king; he was one
who could provide food for hungry people.

Later, when he had the chance, Jesus explained the meaning behind his miracle: *he is the bread of life.* He is the one
Person absolutely basic and essential to life that is rich and
complete. Only if he becomes a part of life does that life enjoy
deep satisfaction.

People in our world need to hear and understand this part of
Christ's message—and of the supper. Many people have a deep,
almost indefinable drive—a gnawing need for something that
they have not been able to provide, something their fellows do
not offer them, and something their world cannot produce. This
has been described as a need for God, a hunger for the eternal, a
God-shaped blank at the center of life. I am convinced that a
fellowship of love and acceptance is available without which we
remain poor, restless, and searching. It is a fellowship that is
offered by the One who made us for himself. Satisfaction,
fulfillment, peace—call it what you will, this desirable attribute of
life often eludes us and will continue to do so apart from Christ.

On one occasion, in a difficult statement to some who followed
him, Jesus indicated dramatically that he is essential to real life. In
John 6:54, Jesus said: "Whoso eateth my flesh . . . hath eternal life."
He said that he was the living bread and that people must eat of that
bread. Of course, these words cannot be subjected to a crude
literalism. *Jesus was talking about assimilation.* He and his principles
for life must become integral parts of every life, just as bread that is
eaten and digested becomes part of the body.

In the supper, the men whom Jesus had chosen ate the bread. By doing so *they reaffirmed their assimilation of Jesus and his principles into their lives.* The message of the supper is that this is not only possible, but it is also imperative. The truth then is restated by a second act.

Jesus used a second basic ingredient that commonly was included in the meals of his day. The disciples performed the symbolic act of drinking the "fruit of the vine" (Matt. 26:29) from a common cup. As they did so, he said that this symbolized his blood, his life, which he would give to seal a new covenant between God and responsive people.

At the beginning of his ministry, Jesus had changed water to wine. He had done this, not merely to ensure the success of a marriage feast in Cana, but primarily to give objective expression to the basic purpose of his whole ministry. He was bringing something new to people's lives, something much better than what had gone before. He had come to bring new life that was and is made possible by God's grace.

Later, when he talked about people eating his flesh, he also said that they must drink his blood. Again, we must get past a repulsive literalism to the truth expressed in his words. His life—his kind of life—was and is available. *But it must be appropriated by a willful act of receiving.* This something new that Jesus brought, a relationship of grace, must be received by each individual.

As the disciples drank from the cup, they reaffirmed their desire that relationship to their Lord continue. All but one. *By their act, they restated their appropriation of Christ's kind of life.*

Both elements of the supper, therefore, serve to express the same basic truth. We perform parallel acts which convey one message. The supper proclaims people's imperative need to assimilate the Bread of life, to appropriate full life by a deliberate choice. By partaking of the supper, we reaffirm our choice; and we underline our conviction that choosing Christ is necessary for every person's redemption.

7

The Tenses of the Supper

1 Corinthians 11:23-28

The thought is not original with me. I suppose some preacher in vague antiquity first thought of it and preached it, and it has been handed down—sort of—from preacher to preacher. I refer to the idea that the Lord's Supper causes those of us who participate to look at a past which is our rich heritage, a present in which we are involved, and a future which we can move to meet with confidence.

Paul wrote that, in originating his meal, Jesus took both the bread and the cup and commanded his disciples to partake. After Jesus' death, they were to share the meal in remembrance of him. Paul was indicating to the Corinthian Christians that they were not to meet and to think only of themselves; they were to meet and to reflect on Christ.

I can imagine that to the early Christians, the immediate past was of crucial significance. Some of those who were present at the Lord's Supper celebrations could remember what Jesus had said and done on specific occasions. Some who were present had spoken with eyewitnesses. They looked closely at the past, taking out treasured memories and examining them once again for the inspiration that they offered.

But I think that their look at the past centered on Jesus' final hours: the night in the upper room, the garden of Gethsemane, the betrayal, the arrest, the trial, the crucifixion, and the resurrection. In some sense, they relived this past through the medium of faith. And I imagine that the early Christians left their meeting place charged once again by the knowledge of what Christ had given to them: new life at the cost of his own.

We come to the Master's meal to look back, not with growing nostalgia, but with joy and appreciation. We look back at a past that was recorded for us in the pages of the New Testament. It is a past over which is written in large letters the word *REDEMP-TION*. And once again we look with eyes of understanding at God's purpose for people, his compassion for all persons, his involvement in real struggle to reclaim us. We look back at an event which reaches outside our ability to understand.

But our looking at the past is meaningful only if it causes us to come to grips with the present. The Lord's Supper is not merely a session in history. It is an incentive to our proper use of the present. Paul reminded the Corinthian Christians that by participation in the supper, they showed the Lord's death until his coming again. The word translated "shew" in the King James Version literally means to announce, to proclaim, to celebrate. In essence, the early Christians were supposed to be bearing a witness by their participation in the supper. In this recreated context, they were testifying to the effectiveness of Christ's death and resurrection for their own lives. In a real sense, our participation in this meal is a proclamation—a celebration—of the essentials of the good news: Christ's life given for every person, his ability to transform and sustain. Participation in the supper is the individual Christian's announcement that, to him or her, Christ's life, death, and resurrection comprise the center point of all history—and demand every person's most crucial decision.

In addition to proclamation by participation, our presence at this meal constitutes a celebration of the Lord who lives. We normally look on Easter as the time when we emphasize Christ's continuing presence. In reality, every time we gather to worship, we celebrate this fact; some people celebrate each day in their awareness of One who is with them. But we emphasize this truth every time we eat together at the Lord's table. He lives as our contemporary, giving strength and leadership for the demands of the present. He is here, not as a ghost, but in his people. The supper makes the present a time of proclamation and celebration.

And the supper causes us to look to the future. Paul wrote: you proclaim, or celebrate, the Lord's death *until he comes.* Those early Christians met together to share this meal with a sense of expectancy. They reviewed the past and saw the opportunities of the present. But they also looked to the future with assurance. No matter what current appearances might have been, the future already was certain. They would carry on as best they could until the Lord's return. No *if* was involved in their thinking. History was moving toward a climax; God had a purpose for people, and that purpose was moving relentlessly toward fulfillment. God's victory over wrong and death had been won with his Son's death on the cross and the Son's resurrection from the dead. The triumph of good over evil was no longer in question; the only question was on what side individuals would align themselves. That still remains life's most crucial question.

The future, then, belongs to God. We can move confidently to encounter tomorrow, knowing that God awaits at the end. He has been active in the past, works now, and stands at history's climax.

God help us to include all the tenses of the Lord's Supper—past, present, and future—so that the meal's inclusive nature may be an enlightening and strengthening experience for us.

8

Supper of Fellowship

I Corinthians 10:16

In chapter 10 of 1 Corinthians, Paul issued a stern warning to Christians living in pagan environments. They were not to participate in feasts held in honor of idols; to do so would identify them with those who worshiped the idols. In making his strong statements, Paul referred to the Lord's Supper; and he used a suggestive term. The King James Version translates the word "communion"; thus, one designation of the Lord's Supper is "Holy Communion." The word employed is *koinōnia*, which indicates joint participation in that which is common to two or more. The word has been rendered "partnership." The most common translation is "fellowship."

Paul was reminding the Corinthian Christians forcefully that the Lord's Supper expresses one's fellowship with Christ and with others. A pagan feast would carry the same implications of relationship. Did they really want to share in anything which gave indications of fellowship with a pagan god and his mistaken followers?

In issuing a warning to Christians of his day, Paul provided a helpful reminder for us. Our coming together to participate in Christ's meal is an open expression of deep, genuine, meaningful fellowship. The first supper was instituted, in part, to emphasize fellowship. It was designed, I am convinced, as a continuing encouragement and challenge to the kind of healthy relationships which must characterize Christ's church.

But wait just a minute! Hold on! We are all different. We come from different backgrounds. We don't think alike, and we don't act the same. We have varying degrees of commitment to Christ and his work, and we don't always agree in matters concerning the church. What do we mean when we say that our coming together is a concrete expression of fellowship? We come—or we should—as those who put foremost in our lives our joint participation in Christ's redemptive work. Lewis Rhodes expressed this truth well: in observing the Lord's Supper, we come to be *with* people and to show that we are *for* people; this is part of what being truly human and genuinely Christian means.

Look closely at the group reclining at the table in the upper room. One would be hard pressed to find a more diverse band of men. Four of them were fishermen; one was a tax collector; one was a member of a radical political party bent on overthrowing Roman rule by force; for reasons of his own, one was about to betray the Lord of life. Among these men were Simon the loud and impetuous; Andrew the quiet; James and John, the "sons of thunder"; Philip the slow to understand; and Thomas the courageous and inquiring. But even in this group of such glaring contrasts, fellowship was the dominant note. For all but one enjoyed fellowship with Christ and were bound together by their mutual participation in his cause.

Try as we may, I don't think that we can get Judas out of the upper room before the Lord's Supper. Luke was explicit at this point. After recording the sharing of the bread and the cup, in 22:21 Luke quoted Jesus as saying: "Behold, the hand of him that betrayeth me is with me on the table." In this statement and in John's poignant scene in which Jesus gave the sop to Judas (John 13:26), Jesus offered fellowship with himself one last time to one who never really had responded. One factor that is striking to me in the setting of the Lord's Supper is the emphasis on a dual fellowship: fellowship with Christ and with those who follow him, and the offer of fellowship to those who are on the outside by choice.

And so, just as the first disciples did, we come to this event signifying deepest fellowship as those who are ordinary, faulty, and imperfect. But we are invited to come by the Lord who knew that we would need reminders of and encouragement to fellowship. Imperfect as it was, the early church strengthened its fellowship through the shared meal. In Acts 2:42, Luke reported that the early Christians "continued steadfastly in the apostles' doctrine and fellowship, and in breaking of bread, and in prayers." The terms "fellowship" and "breaking of bread" probably are to be taken together; the meal that they shared pointed to relationship.

I was helped by being reminded that the Passover, the Jewish celebration of release from Egypt which provided the setting in which the Lord's Supper originated, was celebrated by families. This symbolized an unbroken fellowship of those who formed one body with the God who had passed over the blood-sprinkled doors. So, the fellowship we celebrate in this meal is like that of a family at its highest and best, with its unbroken, essential solidarity. God is Father, and we are his children. We are related through grace and are working in the same redemptive purpose. It is a fellowship of mutual love, trust, and acceptance.

And so, we come to participate in a meal given to us. We come as forgiven people invited into fellowship with a gracious God. We come as those privileged to be related to one another in the work which is ours as God's people sharing in the world's greatest enterprise. May the fellowship that we celebrate be the mark of our lives as we live and work in community.

9

Supper of Thanksgiving

Matthew 26:26-30

Death literally waited outside the door of the upper room where Jesus was eating with his disciples. Jesus was nearing his encounter with treachery, hatred, and violence. But first, he had determined to observe the Passover with those closest to him. After the Passover observance, he instituted a new meal for his church. In the course of the meal, he paused twice to give thanks. I have often wondered what he said in giving thanks on this particular occasion. Some have suggested that he repeated the usual Jewish formula: "Blessed art thou, O Lord our God, king of the world, who dost bring forth bread from the earth."[1] I would like to think that although Jesus' thanks may have included this statement, his prayer was more spontaneous and wider in scope. I would like to think that his expression included his disciples and the events about to take place. The amazing thing in this crisis— outside of Jesus' calmness and assurance—is that in moments of chilling threat, Jesus gave thanks.

But then, Jesus' giving thanks, even in crisis, ought not to be surprising. A study of his life reveals that gratitude was an outstanding feature of it. We are given repeated instances in which Jesus expressed his thanks. A number of such instances had to do with food. Before the feedings of the five thousand and the four thousand, he gave thanks. Before eating with the disciples he had accompanied on the road to Emmaus after his resurrection, he gave thanks; in fact, this characteristic practice caused them finally to recognize him. Before he called Lazarus from the tomb, he gave thanks for the power of God that was about to be revealed. So during his ministry, Jesus expressed his gratitude for simple things, such as food; and he gave thanks for the Father's presence and power.

Because of his total life, and particularly because he gave thanks for the bread and the fruit of the vine as he gave his followers a meal to observe, Jesus made thanksgiving an integral part of what we now commonly call the Lord's Supper. One of the terms used to designate this meal is "The Eucharist," which means the thanksgiving. Thus, each time that we meet together to participate in this meal, we make it an experience of reverent gratitude. All collective worship periods and private devotional periods are times for expressing gratitude, but this is especially true of the Lord's Supper. Part of what we do is to express our deep appreciation to God. George Buttrick wrote that this giving of thanks should spread over all of life and our whole world, " for the whole creation is sacramental, but it [our giving of thanks] should focus in . . . Christ."[2] Our thanksgiving centers around the Person who shows us God.

In the Eucharist or Lord's Supper, *we offer thanks for Christ's selfless life and atoning death.* We acknowledge that our reconciliation to God is not the product of our own effort, but the result of God's working on our behalf. We can do nothing less than express gratitude for the towering truth expressed so eloquently by Christ's life and death: before we thought of loving God, he loved us. John wrote in his first letter: "Herein is love, not that we loved God, but that he loved us, and sent his Son to be the propitiation [expiation] for our sins" (4:10). Before we were good, lovely, or gracious, God in his goodness gave of himself to us. Before we desired to relate to him, he sought to bring us to himself. In the Eucharist, we give thanks for Christ and his self-giving, and we echo the words of Paul in 2 Corinthians 9:15: "Thanks be unto God for his unspeakable gift."

In the course of participation in the Lord's Supper, *we offer thanks for the resurrection, that event which marked the completion of God's redemptive work for us.* The resurrection is the historical fact which offers irrefutable evidence that God *was* in Christ reconciling the world to himself. We look back at the resurrection as evidence that God is able to thwart the attempts of evil to hold the upper hand in life and as evidence that God is capable of giving life. We look back in gratitude at the resurrection because it validates Christ's words and deeds. We view the resurrection with thanksgiving because of the promise it holds for us of life beyond death. But most of all, we look to the resurrected Lord who shows himself to be the Lord of life, One who is living, present, powerful in our todays. He is One who grants triumph over life, wrong, and death to those of faith. And again, we humbly echo Paul's words in 1 Corinthians 15:57: "Thanks be to God, which giveth us the victory."

By our participation in the Eucharist, *we express our gratitude for the church's beginning and continuation in Christ's life.* The church's foundation is God's grace seen in Christ's self-giving. The example by which the church orders its life is his life. The message the church proclaims is that Christ gives life.

In this meal, we express our awareness of and our thanks for *the Commission that our resurrected Lord gave to his church*: the charge to make disciples of all people and to nurture them in the faith.

Also, we openly thank God for the gracious promise which accompanies his Commission, the promise that we do not labor in our strength alone. He sustains his work by his presence with his church. His church works in the confidence that it will be victorious; it shares and will share his triumph.

And so, we participate in the Eucharist, the Lord's Supper, with a prayer of thanksgiving. We not only look back in gratitude for what Christ has accomplished at Golgotha, on the first Easter morning, and in the early church, but also we offer our thanks for what he is doing now in his people's lives and in his church's life and ministry.

NOTES
1. Sherman E. Johnson, *The Interpreter's Bible*, Vol. 7 (Nashville: Abingdon Press, 1951), p. 575.
2. George Buttrick, Ibid., p. 576.

10

Supper of Assurance

Mark 14:25; Matthew 26:29

Sometimes, I try to imagine the early church's participation in the Lord's Supper. I find myself wishing that somehow we could recapture some of the excitement and deep meaning that this meal held for Christians living and ministering in a hostile environment. They met to keep this meal because their Lord had commanded that they do so; they met to remember his words and acts, especially those of the night on which he was betrayed and arrested. Further, they met to celebrate his powerful presence in their midst. This shared meal had meaning that one outside the Christian fellowship could not begin to understand.

But I am convinced that the early Christians met and ate the Lord's meal together for another reason. *They met together in order to gain assurance and encouragement for the hard and dangerous adventure of being Christ's followers.* I can see them as they exhorted one another, as they shared their experiences, and as they gave support by listening in sympathetic friendship. But I think they gained their greatest assurance—a renewed confidence which sent them out to face severe threats with courage—from something Jesus said that night in the upper room before his arrest and death.

The more I think about the scene, the more incredible it becomes. Jesus stood on the edge of the dark chasm of a crisis which would end in his death. Human hounds were dogging his steps, intent on spilling his blood. Jesus had arranged for a final few hours alone with his disciples in order that he might attempt to prepare them for what was coming immediately—and beyond. One thing was certain in his mind: the terrible Roman cross awaited him. Now, unless we make Jesus' real humanity a game of "let's pretend," dying at the hands of those who hated him was an experience filled with all the agony and threat imaginable. Indeed, such an experience was even more agonizing for One who was giving himself up voluntarily in order to draw people to God. We can turn over a few pages in the New Testament and read about the resurrection; we can turn to the last verses of Luke or the first chapter of Acts and read about the ascension. But to One living the drama of redemption, what loomed ahead for sure was a cross and a tomb.

But let me go back a minute. I said that one thing, death, was certain in Jesus' mind there in the upper room. Actually, two things were certain to him. The other was that *beyond his death, God's purpose would win*. For in talking with his disciples, he said something about drinking no more fruit of the vine until the time when he would drink it fresh in the kingdom of God. His words betrayed his thoughts: he had no doubt that God's activity in his world on behalf of people would come out as God meant for it to come out. Nothing or nobody could prevent God from realizing his redemptive purpose.

From the tone and content of Jesus' conversation, this meal was no final farewell! A note of sadness was in his words, for the former relationship with his apostles was to end soon. He no longer would walk the dusty trails of Palestine with them; he no longer would teach them, discipline them, and inspire them by his unusual deeds. But instead of farewell, the time in the upper room was a time of beginning again. Instead of defeat, what was about to happen on Golgotha would be victory! Beyond the events about to descend so rapidly and with such crushing force, much more was to come.

The disciples were familiar with the Jewish belief in a messianic banquet at the end of the age. The Last Supper was both a foretaste of that kind of fellowship and a pledge that no matter how present circumstances might appear, Jesus' separation from his disciples was only temporary. On the other side of seeming defeat would be glorious triumph. On the far side of death awaited a third day and resurrection.

Halford Luccock wrote that because of Jesus' confidence in ultimate victory, because of his reassuring words in the darkest of hours, the Lord's Supper was a celebration to the early Christians. It was a joyous occasion—not a look back at tragedy, "but a looking forward to victory and the consummation of a kingdom."[1]

As we come to place ourselves in the context of Christ's suffering and dying for us, his words speak to us. Again, Halford Luccock affirmed that dark hours occur in everybody's experience. Dark hours come in the history of civilization. When these hours come, he wrote, "The only life possible is life with an immanent sense of death at the door."[2] Then people easily drift into a defeatist attitude. In our times of personal doubt and sense of defeat, we need the reassurance of Christ's words which expressed his own deep, personal confidence.

A touching revelation to me as a parent has been that children sometimes come to their parents wanting nothing more than a reassuring touch or word—proof that the parents are still there and still love them and that everything is going to be all right. As humbly as children, we come to these sacred moments to experience the reassuring presence of One who said that he would be with his followers to the end of the age. We come reverently into the presence of One who professed and proved his love by every word and act of his life—and by his death.

We come to have our confidence renewed—our confidence that, no matter what present indications may seem to be, we are aligned with God's victorious push in history. We who follow Christ are on the winning team because on the other side of difficulties, dangers, threats, and failures is ultimate victory through our capable Leader. He is the Pioneer of our salvation, the Author and Finisher of our faith.

Despite all of its problems from without and from within, the church will be led to triumph. Its strength is not to be traced to human sources but to God who wills to use it as an instrument of redemption.

And so, we come to participate in the Lord's Supper in order to strengthen our confidence in the victory of love over wrong, assured by the God who does not fail. And we come to express our gratitude that our lives have been given that creative assurance.

NOTES
1. Halford Luccock, *The Interpreter's Bible*, Vol. 7, p. 878.
2. Ibid.

11

Supper of Expectancy

Matthew 26:26-29

The stark truth merits our reflection: the Last Supper was not a gesture of farewell but a pledge of ultimate victory. Jesus promised his disciples and all those who would place their trust in him through the ages that a reunion of his people would take place in a context of celebration. I like the way Matthew recorded this promise of Jesus: "I will not drink henceforth of this fruit of the vine, until that day when I drink it new with you in my Father's kingdom" (26:29).

I attempted in a previous Lord's Supper meditation to center on the notes of assurance and confidence in this statement. From the moment Jesus spoke the words, his followers have drawn encouragement from them. I also have tried to emphasize the fact that the supper looks forward to final triumph; the meal has a future tense. The future belongs to God and will see the culmination of his high purpose. Beyond these truths is the additional factor of *expectancy* present in the celebration of the meal. We can gather to celebrate the Lord's Supper in a mood of expectancy concerning what God is going to do ultimately. Moreover, we can contemplate what he is going to do in and through us in moments of worship and in days of living. We can live our lives in an attitude of expectancy.

Numerous people have said many times that one reason some of us derive so little or nothing from periods of collective worship is that we come together expecting little or nothing. What Nels Ferre wrote about prayer is true of worship. He wrote that we must pray expectantly and that if our hopes in Christ "do not extend beyond our natural expectations, we might as well not pray."[1] We most definitely do not worship when we do not expect something from God. What we receive may be a phrase from someone's prayer that strikes a responsive chord. It may be a hymn or a line from a song that lifts our spirits. A word from Scripture or a thought embedded in a sermon may begin to speak to a need. The handshakes and evident openness of fellow members of the company may offer support or encouragement. If we come expectantly, openly, God will speak or move.

Several years ago, I had entered the Sunday morning worship period more expectantly than in previous Sundays; I had keen anticipation, for I desperately wanted to be a prophetic spokesman that morning. I wanted God to use what was done in that worship period to have significant impact on some lives. I sat listening to the special music prior to the sermon. One line repeated in the song put me in touch with a basic tenet of my personal faith, and gratitude from the depths of my life sought expression. I received something of value; I experienced worship because I had a degree of expectancy in my approach to that period designated for collective worship. We should come to this unique celebration expecting deep to answer to deep.

In fact, of all the times we gather for worship, the times we meet to participate in Christ's supper should be approached with high expectation. Through something meaningful that he has given to his people, *we should expect Christ to speak some redemptive, creative word.* Just as Jesus spoke words of redemption, of his self-giving, on that night long ago, so we should come anticipating that some words prompting to salvation will be spoken again. In the recreated, historical context of Jesus' choosing to give himself for all people and for each person, we should expect to hear God saying that what is dearest to him— most vital—is the redemption of persons. We should hear him saying that he goes on giving of himself so that every person might have an opportunity to respond and become his.

We ought to come to celebrate Christ's meal expecting the Creator of the universe and the Creator of our selves to move within our lives. If we invite him to be present personally with us, he will be. If we reflect on his awesome majesty, holiness, graciousness, and love for each of us, then he can move us to new repentance, commitment, and vitality in our relationships to him. How long has it been since you have been moved deeply by anything that you have experienced in collective worship? Have you been moved by music, prayer, a truth of Scripture, or the presence of some fellow member of the company who is battling courageously through crisis or whose life breathes Christ's spirit? Although I try to avoid manipulating people by sheer emotionalism, I know the experience of being moved to greater openness to God, to empathy, and to praise. Jesus was moved to compassion, sorrow, anger, and love. We should come to his meal expecting to experience his moving us to deeper relationships to him and to each other. We must be sensitive to the impulses of his presence.

We should come to the Lord's Supper celebration expecting the quality of our life together as a Christian community to be enriched. Confronted with the reminders that we come to his table, that we are his people, and that we share a unique relationship, we should receive impetus toward the creation of a stronger spirit of unity. Meditating in the context of Christ's self-sacrifice, we ought to make progress toward putting his redemptive thrust through his church first and our needs to control, manipulate, and direct aside. I cannot understand how we can come together repeatedly to celebrate the supper and fail to examine our proneness to self-interest and self-assertion and to be convicted for it. I need to come back to the concept of adding my efforts to yours in the creation of cohesiveness and stronger influence as Christ's people. Some of us need to be drawn again to that idea, that truth. We ought to come expecting God to use us in the coordinated functioning of his body.

Long ago, James indicated to his readers that they did not have because they did not ask. Perhaps we don't receive from worship what we need because we really do not expect to do so. The celebration of the Lord's Supper could be a time when we receive spiritual strength, if we come anticipating God's response to our asking.

NOTE
1. Nels F. S. Ferré, *Making Religion Real* (New York: Harper & Brothers Publishers, 1955), p. 65.

12

Supper of Sharing

1 Corinthians 10:16-17

The New Testament writers present us with a number of beautiful scenes from Christ's life. We are allowed to see him as he helped the helpless, brought hope to the despairing, offered redemption to the sinful, and shared his life with the twelve he chose to be with him. We watch as he loved, gave, and agonized over those who refused to respond. We are privileged to see the beauty of his manhood, Godlike manhood—ultimate humanity, and true godliness focused in one man.

No scene in Christ's life is more beautiful than the one in which he shared some of his final moments with his disciples over a meal. He was nearing the supreme crisis in his life; he knew his death was inevitable. Yet, in a spirit of fellowship which danger could not disrupt and death could not end, Christ did something beautiful for his disciples and for all disciples through the centuries. He shared a meal with his men, and he left this meal for all his people in all ages to share.

Christ's meal expresses the attitude, the mind-set, in which Christ's followers must share. The Lord's Supper demands what Paul demanded of the Philippian Christians: "Let this mind be in you, which was also in Christ Jesus" (Phil. 2:5). We are called on to have a persistent love that gives itself in serving people. Halford Luccock declared that we cannot avoid the question the Lord's meal asks. The supper first affirms that Jesus' life, given voluntarily, was his "blood of the new testament, . . . shed for many" (Mark 14:24). Then the supper asks: "Are your life, your blood, your strength, poured out at all?"[1]

Christ's meal is the supper of sharing. As we participate together, we are reminded that our following Christ is a continuous experience of sharing.

The supper was instituted in a context of Christ's death. Although he died alone, between two thieves, rejected by his own people, virtually abandoned by his disciples, his meal reminds us that our entrance into relationship with him comes only *by our sharing his death*. Paul expressed this truth in Romans 6:3: "Know ye not, that so many of us as were baptized into Jesus Christ were baptized into his death?" Our old man is crucified with him, Paul argued; we experience a change from our former selves so radical that it can be described best as dying to sin. Not only that but also Christ's death becomes the principle by which we live. He gave himself for us; we give ourselves to him and to others. He died for us, true enough. But we become his people only by sharing his death.

Christ's meal reminds us that *we share a priceless gift*. We share the gift of redemption, the gift of a new life. Once we groveled in the squalor of our spiritual poverty, whether or not we realized it. But now we sit at the King's table; we live from his bounty; we receive from his benevolent hand. We share the experience of receiving that which we could not produce for ourselves, gain in trade, or receive as remuneration for labor. We share the sheer gift given by a gracious God—a gift of his love, a gift for which we can make no repayment. We cannot repay a gift of grace.

In Mobile, Alabama, after an automobile accident, my wife Barbara had to be confined to bed for an extended period. I had to work at my job on the staff of a church. People came by our apartment with food; some of them washed dishes; several checked on Barbara from time to time. A lawyer volunteered his services; people called during the day to see how things were going. I remarked to one lady, in essence: "I don't know how we will ever repay all the gracious things you ladies have done for us."

"You can't repay us," she said matter-of-factly. "But you may have a chance someday to do something like this for someone else."

We cannot repay a gift of grace, *but such a gift can move us to give.* We share God's gift of himself, and we share the sheer joy of giving to others in his name.

And so, *we share service together*—Christian service, self-less service. We engage in constructive efforts designed to lift others, acts designed to express Christ's love in language that they can understand—actions done specifically to articulate God's care in concrete terms. We share a ministry to every person in need within our reach. The cup of cold water, the piece of bread, the article of clothing, the words of encouragement and comfort, the listening ear, the strengthening presence—we have the marvelous privilege of being Christ's hands and feet, swift to help.

In our shared service, we discover that *we are sharing God's life.* We share triumph and tragedy, success and failure, joy and sorrow, correctness and mistake. Because we are the church in action in every area of life, we enjoy the discovery that God intends for us to live together and to share his life.

Part of our shared life is the rewarding *sharing of worship together.* Many of us worship individually, reading the Scriptures and praying, but we meet together to seek the mind of God. We seek to think his thoughts after him and to do his commandments. Shared worship moves us to the realization that all of us are in the same bundle. Shared worship, and especially the Lord's meal, forges a bond between us. We are a community sharing Christ's power, presence, and imperatives. We share in advancement under his leadership.

In the meal long ago, Christ shared bread and the fruit of the vine with his disciples; more than that, he shared himself and his conclusive triumph with them. He continues to share with us. And we share with one another; we share his death, his gift, his ministry, his life, and worship. His meal reminds us of the depth of our sharing.

NOTE
1. Luccock, *T.I.B.*, Vol. 7, p. 877.

13

Supper of Invitation

Matthew 26:26-29

The evening of Jesus' life, the twilight of his brief public ministry, had begun. Events now were rushing with ever-increasing pace toward trial, crucifixion, and resurrection. Jesus had arranged for one last quiet, private meeting with his disciples. They ate together in an upper room. At the end of the regular meal, in a simple and yet meaningful manner, Jesus chose two of the meal's ingredients to symbolize his sacrificial death and the new relationship between God and people which this death would make accessible. After he took the loaf, broke it, and gave thanks, his first words to his disciples were words of invitation: "Take, eat." Jesus was offering them food, symbolic of something far more significant. He was offering these men his fellowship, his companionship, his redemptive life. Only by his invitation could they participate in what he was making available. Only because he chose to include them could they become foundation stones of his church.

When we meet together to participate in Christ's meal, by what we do we portray the announcement beyond compare: God extends a continuing invitation to people, an invitation to life.

God has made himself known as majestic, holy, and able— One who is worthy of worship. But he also has shown himself to be the gracious God who invites. He selected a people to be uniquely his; they were to enjoy the privilege of special revelation so that they might fulfill the responsibility of making God known and of inviting all people to become members of his commonwealth. His purpose in inviting Israel to follow him was to issue through his chosen people an open invitation to everyone. In Isaiah 55:1, God's prophet saw this clearly and spelled it out to his people: "Ho, every one that thirsteth, come ye to the waters, and he that hath no money; come ye, buy, and eat; yea, come, buy wine and milk without money and without price."

Jesus voiced the same invitation in Matthew 11:28: "Come unto me, all ye that labor and are heavy laden, and I will give you rest." He invited all sorts of people: the Pharisee in his spiritual pride; the publican in his extortion; the common, poor people. Jesus invited people *to come and receive, to come and become, to come and be enabled to give.* In the last chapter of the last book of the Bible, the invitation is repeated: "And the Spirit and the bride [the church] say, Come. And let him that heareth say, Come. And let him that is athirst come. And whosoever will, let him take the water of life freely" (Rev. 22:17). God has revealed himself as One who invites people to himself.

The Jews made God's invitation a closed one, only for a particular, preferred few. They envisioned a messianic banquet when Messiah came to usher in God's kingdom, his new age. Of course, every Jew would be present. All others would be left out. During his ministry, Jesus warned that God does not exclude people. God does not make up a guest list of preferred persons. He does not invite just those who have been friendly to him, those who have done him favors, or those who are likable. He does not just invite those who are most useful to him. Jesus told vivid stories about people who prepared great banquets and invited others to come. These stories included refusal by some and acceptance by the most unlikely guests. Jesus was saying that one must respond to God's invitation, and one must recognize the seriousness and importance of the invitation when it comes.

Here it is, Jesus said in so many words to his disciples in the upper room: the messianic banquet in miniature. Truly the supper is the kingdom meal. And it is based on two simple ingredients, given by Jesus' invitation. We call this the "Lord's Supper," and rightly so. He originated it for his church; he gave it meaning by giving himself; and he is the One who invites every person to take part. Only he can invite.

We must guard against participating in this worship experience casually or with a familiarity which robs it of its freshness. We review Christ's invitation, which many of us have accepted. He has invited because only he can give the gift of redemption. Only he could offer the perfect sacrifice. Only the Lord of life can identify himself with all of our human needs. We receive from his hands the gifts of grace. We acknowledge that we are here because Christ has invited.

But the supper of invitation also reminds us that we are to extend God's invitation. We are his church, and our central task is to issue his invitation. We articulate his loving summons to those whose hunger can be satisfied only by the Bread of life, to those who need the care of the Good Shepherd. *We invite because we have been given the privilege of inviting.* We can invite the wrong to receive Christ's forgiveness, the guilty to receive his grace, the sinful to receive his mercy. "Take, this is for you," we can say.

And so, we are reminded again that at the heart of the Christian experience are an extended invitation on God's part and a receiving on our part. First, before God expects anything from us, commands something of us, or makes something of us, he asks that we receive. "Take," he says, "this is for you."

The Lord's Supper is a graphic portrayal of the truth that God invites all people to his table; room is available for every person in his boundless provision. Those who respond in faith may come. The fact that we participate is proof that God is no respecter of persons in his continuing invitation.

14

Correcting a Misconception

Mark 14:22-26

One of the tragedies in the life of Christ's church in our day centers around the general attitude toward the Lord's Supper. Unfortunately, many people feel that this experience is a departure from the normal in Christian worship. Pastors must share the responsibility for this gross error. Often, the supper is tacked on to the end of a service, is participated in hastily, and is not given the atmosphere of reverence that it deserves. Instead of occupying the center of the stage, it is pushed off to one side. Some congregations have received little explanation of the meal—its significance, its meaning, and correct participation by the Lord's people. Therefore, if church members are going to deliberately miss one worship period, many feel that they can be absent from the Lord's Supper. After all, it soon becomes "old hat." The participants listen to often-repeated and familiar Scriptures. They go through the same motions: they chew on a little piece of dry cracker and drink a small amount of grape juice. The whole thing becomes an exercise in boredom, and many people find themselves hoping that it won't take too long. And so, what difference does it make if they miss this departure from the regular worship periods?

I contend that such an attitude is a tragedy because it deprives a person of what can be one of the most profoundly meaningful and effective worship experiences that he or she will know. Approached with reverence and expectation, and participated in prayerfully, the Lord's Supper can cause Christ's presence with his people to be felt as at few other times.

Ironically, one of the strange developments in the church has been the necessity of promoting the Lord's Supper. We are finding that we must urge people to come or to "stay for church" after Sunday School to participate in the Lord's meal. This would have been incredible to the early disciples. How could anyone not want to take part in this act given to the church by the church's Lord? If, somehow, they could observe our usual custom, they would be surprised that we do not eat together more as a fellowship. And they would be perplexed at our participation in Christ's meal once a quarter or once a month. Most likely, they ate and drank in remembrance of Christ each time they gathered; such an act was a vital part of their fellowship in worship. Glen Hinson has suggested that one key to deeper fellowship in our churches may be a more frequent participation in the Lord's Supper. The early church joyfully anticipated this meal as an act of sincere worship.

As Christ's people, we should anticipate the Master's meal *because the church never worships more genuinely than at this time.* Worship is the response of one's whole being to the God who is interested in the total person. It is opening life to One whose love can correct and strengthen. It is committing life anew to One who can nurture, develop, and use it in his high purpose. The supper was designed as an objective expression of just such an experience and expression.

All the elements of true worship are here: sincere thanksgiving for blessings received and anticipated; confession of wrongs committed and redemptive acts left undone; petition for creative forgiveness; dedication to service; witness to one's faithfulness to the fellowship. The supper can be a periodic experience of renewal in one's Christian living. It can become an avenue for repeated commitment.

The supper is a concrete expression of our identification with Christ and his church; it gives renewed awareness of his power to accomplish what he has promised, and to do it through people; it serves as a reminder that we are engaged in his ministry.

Never are we more conscious of what God has done, is doing, and will do than when we are participating in Christ's meal. The meal provides a consciousness of God which we need desperately.

We should look forward to the Lord's Supper *because, by participating, we come as close as we will come to imitating an actual act of Christ.* He left two acts which he explicitly commanded that we keep: baptism and the Lord's Supper. The design for these two creative experiences came from the Savior's mind. We literally are following in his steps in at least two points.

We cannot go back to the upper room, to those crisis-laden hours. But we can recreate the moment in history. We are obeying Christ concretely, for all to see. Thus, our desire to participate should be an indication of our willingness to obey him at other points in our living.

Our willing absence, our take-it-or-leave-it attitude, our careless and casual participation all point to deeper disobedience and unconcern. These are surface indications of deeper difficulties in our relationship to Christ. These indicate an apathy eating away at our inner lives—a lethargy which threatens our usefulness and effectiveness.

You and I correct the misconception concerning the Lord's Supper by allowing it to have proper significance in our lives, by allowing it to be a renewing worship experience.

15

Impetus to Community

1 Corinthians 10:16

One of the terms that is used to designate the Lord's supper is the word *Communion*. According to *Webster's New World Dictionary of the English Language*, our English word can mean "a sharing, possession in common, participation, an intimate spiritual relationship." In 1 Corinthians 10:16, the word *Communion* translates a Greek term which designates a joint participation in that which is common to two or more persons. The term *Communion* belongs to the same family as the word *community*. The Lord's Supper, then, is the common meal of God's community. It is a reminder of, and a challenge to, meaningful community.

People have held, and hold now, varying views of how the Lord's Supper should be celebrated. Many have definite ideas about the people who should take part. Some hold that only the members of the local Baptist church are eligible to participate. This is called "closed communion." Others feel that all those who have committed their lives to Christ, no matter what their denomination might be, can participate in the Lord's Supper celebration. This is called "open communion."

Whatever view of the Lord's Supper we hold, when we meet to celebrate together we come face-to-face with a sobering truth: we have a great deal in common. We have some things in common with all of the people who ever lived and who live now: joys, sorrows, hopes, dreams, and aspirations. Especially do we have some experiences in common with those who respond to Christ in faith. We are related by grace to others who have responded to Christ in a faith commitment. In community, you and I have a commonality that is creative. Look with me at some of the things that we have in common.

We share an awareness of our weaknesses. In our good moments, when we think clearly and seriously, we realize that we are people who have wrong in common, who experience repeated failures and spiritual lapses, who lack the spiritual competence that we know we ought to have. And we recognize that we are not capable of coping with all those things which thrust their way into our experience. We are people whose abilities, resources, and moral strength are limited.

We have something else in common: *a recognition that we have been, and continue to be, the recipients of a forgiveness to which we have no proper claim, no right for which we can press.* We are related in that we share an experience of receiving grace. We are fellow members of the family of the forgiven; we are sinners who have found pardon and a sustaining love. And we are those who regard people beyond the church as potential recipients of the same forgiveness which can recreate and enable them. Our communion with each other as Christians, and with all people, is based on a deep desire that all persons understand and appropriate forgiveness that is available and is offered by One who loves every person.

Furthermore, *we participate in a common struggle to gain the personhood that we glimpse in Christ.* We are involved in a never-ending effort to move on from where we know ourselves to be to where every instinct tells us that we should be as persons. We all strive to locate and remove the ugly in our lives with Christ's help. No matter how radical the surgery might be, we ask Christ to remove that which limits and diminishes life. We ask that he replace it with attractive Christlikeness.

Then, *we participate in a common attempt to exercise faith and constantly to enhance its quality by letting it live in what we do.* We try to allow faith to result in works that add to the lives of people around us. We seek to cooperate with God as he works in us to bring our salvation to fulfillment, completion. As Paul expressed in Ephesians 4:4-6a. "There is one body, and one Spirit, even as ye are called in one hope of your calling; One Lord, one faith, one baptism, One God and Father of all."

Thus, to me, the Communion is, in a deep sense, a given meal for those who have been forgiven and who want continuing forgiveness for sins and strength to be more than they are. It is for people who turn their eyes longingly toward the Galilean Carpenter. By participation in this meal, we reaffirm our identification with Christ and with the humanity that he gave himself to redeem. The Lord's Supper is the communion—a common participation—of those who seek what God alone can give: a true humanity which can feel with our fellow human beings.

16

Reminder of Suffering

Mark 14:22-26

The Lord's Supper is far more than merely a memorial service or a reminder. It is a deeply meaningful worship experience in which we recognize the presence of the living Lord in a recreated context of the last hours, the crisis hours, of his physical life. But Jesus did say, "This do in remembrance of me" (Luke 22:19). And so, at least in part, the supper does call to mind the One in whom God expressed himself as fully as he can do so to finite creatures. We are reminded of Jesus' life of love; his ministry of mercy; his voluntary, vicarious death; his triumphant resurrection. One of the functions of the Lord's Supper is *to ensure that we do not forget*, to make certain that our Savior's self-giving never loses its awesomeness, to make sure that the cost of our redemption is not relegated to the commonplace or taken for granted. The supper is a poignant reminder of sacrificial, selfless suffering on our behalf by One who in this manner gave evidence of the kind of unrelenting love he has for us.

The Lord's Supper was instituted in a context of suffering. Jesus was about to be betrayed by one of his chosen band. He would undergo the agony of Gethsemane, in which he submitted himself anew to the divine will. This experience also would point up the terrible aloneness with which he was to endure what was to come. He would be arrested, given a mock trial, condemned unjustly, and handled shamefully. Then he would be crucified. Despite deepest mental and emotional anguish, and approaching physical suffering, Jesus gave a lasting, acted-out experience for his disciples—and, therefore, for his church. Jesus gave something that his people could imitate; they literally could follow his pattern and experience him anew.

Normally, we do not like to think of suffering, pain, or agony. It is not a pleasant subject. But I get the distinct impression that we have come to the point where many of us look on Christ's suffering without being moved or stirred. We seem to think that his suffering was not as severe as it would be for a normal human being. After all, he was God in human flesh; therefore, he had some supernatural resistance to pain, did he not? The New Testament indicates that God-in-flesh gave himself no advantage; therefore, he gave himself no immunity from pain. In fact, because he felt so deeply, because he loved so deeply, because he was completely human, Christ's suffering was far more extreme than yours or mine could be.

During the supper, Jesus broke a loaf of bread and gave it to his disciples, indicating that it signified his body given in death for them. The fruit of the vine that they all drank signified his blood, sealing a new covenant—blood that would be shed in suffering and death, poured out for all people. Thus, in the supper itself, and in the elements used, is the foreshadowing of Jesus' agony of self-giving.

We cannot plumb the depths of Jesus' suffering. We have not suffered so greatly, so we cannot comprehend fully his experience. But we can take note of some of the areas of his agony; we can be reminded of what he willingly endured for us.

One of the basic problems with which we must deal is that of *rejection.* We want to be appreciated, accepted by other people. Serious personality problems arise when individuals find themselves rejected by those around them. At some time, each of us has experienced rejection. *The most severe pain comes when love is refused,* when one attempts to offer oneself out of a desire to do what is best for another person and is turned away. We hurt when we try to give another person something good and fine, to help in some way, and we are rebuffed. When the best we have to offer—an unselfish concern for another's good—is rejected, the suffering which results often is sharper than a blow to the body.

Here, the limited scope of our understanding allows us to grasp only a small part of what Jesus experienced when he was rejected finally by his people. We get a glimpse of his anguish during his ministry in his lament over Jerusalem recorded in Matthew 23:37: "O Jerusalem, Jerusalem, . . . how often would I have gathered thy children together, even as a hen gathereth her chickens under her wings, and yet would not!" Part of Jesus' suffering came as he watched people reject God's love and grace offered in him, refuse that which was for their benefit, stubbornly resist God's attempt to give them himself and life. This anguish was deep and sharp; it was pain for others, not anguish for himself.

One thing for which most of us look when we face crises is someone to share with us and to offer some support. If only we can feel that we are not alone in difficulty and pain, then we receive a measure of strength and encouragement. *But our suffering is compounded when we must endure it alone.* Jesus' suffering was intensified by the defection of his disciples, his friends. Someone has said that, ironically, Jesus was crucified between two thieves, not two disciples. If ever a man died alone, even though viewed by a throng of people, that man was Jesus. *Alone.* The word seems a perfect synonym for pain. Jesus' loneliness was complete: rejection by the people and the defection of his followers. No wonder, according to Mark 15:34, he cried: "My God, my God, why hast thou forsaken me?" These chilling words were wrung from One who felt absolutely alone in the moment of his death.

Added to rejection and loneliness was *the physical suffering of the cross.* Too often, we state glibly that Christ was crucified or that he died for us; and we never pause to contemplate the manner of Christ's death. Death by crucifixion was one of the cruelest, most barbaric, most torturous forms of capital punishment the world has known. The Romans were experts at it; they knew how to nail a person to the cross in such a way that he would suffer agonizing pain before he finally died. Crucifixion was the slow, torturous method of executing a condemned criminal, a slave, or an insurrectionist.

In a consideration of Christ's suffering, we must be impressed with the fact that he suffered voluntarily *on our behalf*. He chose for himself the role of the Suffering Servant of Isaiah, and so the words of Isaiah 53:5 have been viewed as an appropriate description of Jesus: "He was wounded for our transgressions, he was bruised for our iniquities."

As we participate in the Lord's Supper, seated in a comfortable building, secure, we must be reminded that the first supper was shared in a context of suffering. Suffering *for us*.

17

The Seriousness of the Supper

1 Corinthians 11:27-34

I, for one, am glad that the word *unworthily* is an adverb. If it were an adjective. it would be translated "unworthy" and would have to describe the person or persons participating in the Lord's Supper. Then it would describe me perfectly. And you. For, which of us can stand and say that we are worthy to celebrate the Lord's death, resurrection, and presence by means of a meal that he instituted? Who among us can claim to be deserving of the gift of redemption? But Paul was not writing about unworthy people sharing the Lord's meal.

The word must be rendered "unworthily" (v. 27) and must refer to the *manner* in which people participate in the supper. The hard truth is that we can go through each step of the meal, as we now celebrate it, with perfect decorum and yet violate the purpose and deep meaning which it has. Paul took the Lord's Supper seriously. Look at his words. To participate *lightly* is to earn judgment on a wrong act; such insensitive participation, Paul noted, was the reason some in the Corinthian church were weak and sickly and some were dead. This is strong and puzzling language, and it leaves us with questions. But one thing is clear: Paul did not for one minute condone careless participation in the supper.

We need to understand clearly one fact: *the supper is always open to penitent sinners*. The person who is a sinner, knows it, hates it, and wants a new start is welcome at the Lord's table. Our coming to place ourselves in the recreated context of Jesus' supreme crisis faces us with the stark contrast between his sinless perfection and our flawed imperfection. If we are not conscious of our wrong when we come here, we should be when we are presented with Christ's giving of himself for us—and we should be moved to repentance.

"Whosoever shall eat this bread, and drink this cup of the Lord, unworthily, shall be guilty of the body and blood of the Lord," Paul wrote. To absent oneself deliberately from the supper—to decline the Lords' invitation to celebrate his lordship as a fellowship—is a poor choice, at best. But even worse is to participate lightly, carelessly, or unthinkingly. What does being guilty of the body and the blood of the Lord mean? One suggestion which has intense meaning for me is that these words refer to one's numbering oneself with the kind of people who put Christ to death. To make a mockery of his meal, by failing to reflect on its meaning, is to mock Christ and to take one's place with the kind of people who ridiculed him on Golgotha. That is strong stuff. It means that beyond the symbols of the bread and the cup is an experience which must be approached with deepest reverence and open-eyed awareness.

We have to know what we are doing and to value the act. For here, in this simple procedure, we are in the presence of the One who gave the meal—and then gave it the dimension of the sacred by his death. We honor him and celebrate his lordship. And we cannot do it unthinkingly, carelessly.

Someone has noted that neither pastor nor worshiper can add anything to the content of the supper. Nothing we can do will enhance its meaning. But this does not mean that the spirit of the worshiper is unimportant. The attitude of each guest at the Lord's table is crucial. The openness, reverence, self-awareness, and pentitence we bring—or fail to bring—determine the extent to which we are renewed.

Another possible inference is contained in the phrase "guilty of the body and blood of the Lord." Some have seen here a reference to the church as the body of Christ; therefore, Paul well could have meant that if one's attitude toward the Christian fellowship is not right then that person participates unworthily in the meal designed specifically for the church. If one does not value the church, support it, see it as a priority, and love it, then that person makes a meaningless charade of the Lord's Supper. Paul wrote in Ephesians 5:25 that "Christ also loved the church, and gave himself for it." For us to have a lesser devotion to the church, one which allows us to evade self-giving for the church's redemptive mission, is to degrade the Lord's meal. That is strong stuff, but it well could have been in Paul's thought.

But let us be specific. We can use the phrase "the church" and visualize a formless, gray mass of buildings and people. You and I comprise the church. Thus, you and I must come in openness to each other. John wrote that on the night in which Jesus was betrayed, he gave his disciples a new commandment, that they love one another. This means that we cannot come to the Lord's table with cool indifference to each other or toward those outside Christ's company. It means that we cannot share his meal if we have marked any persons off as not worthy of our attention or concern.

I confess that I have those times when I am ready to count people out. To my way of thinking, they give little indication of being the Christians that they claim to be; they don't seem to care for their church; they seem to be highly selective in their relationships to others. But one outstanding truth has made a difference in how I view these people; it has made me slow my hasty sentencing of them. The individuals I encounter inside and outside the church are people for whom Christ died. How can I summarily dismiss one for whom Christ gave himself? And I am driven back repeatedly into the struggle to understand and to love.

We come to these moments as unworthy people. Let us participate in the supper in a worthy manner—as forgiven sinners deeply grateful for the redemption we have received as a gift and aware of our relatedness as persons for whom Christ died.

18

The Act of Receiving

Mark 14:22-23

In the Lord's Supper celebration, we come together to share in one of the most significant acts we do as a church. We come to participate in the Lord's meal. We do not partake of a full meal, as was eaten on the night in which Jesus originated the supper, but we share a condensed version in which symbols aid in a meaningful experience. We come to place emphasis on the fact that it is *his* meal and, thus, to reaffirm his lordship in our lives.

In our gathering to worship in this special manner, we repeat Jesus' acts on that historic night long ago. After first having expressed gratitude to God, we pass, take, and eat unleavened bread. Again, in an attitude of prayer, we pass, take, and drink the fruit of the vine. We sing a hymn. And then we go out, hopefully with a new awareness of who we are and what we are to do in giving ourselves in service.

In our participation in Christ's meal, whether we recognize it or not, we do something which is at the heart of our relationship to Christ and which enables us to minister in his name. Notice what Mark recorded about the supper: Jesus took bread, blessed it, and offered it to his disciples with the words: "Take, eat." He took his cup, blessed it, and gave it to them; and they all drank of its contents. Involved were the simple acts of giving and receiving, of offering and taking. Of course, Jesus' acts were symbolic of his offering himself, his life, and his work to those twelve men gathered in the upper room. His acts also were symbolic of his offering himself to every person. In addition, of tremendous importance were the disciples' acts in receiving the bread and the fruit of the vine, in taking what Jesus offered. Not only did they acknowledge their readiness to take part in his continuing work, with its demands and challenges but also they acknowledged that Jesus was the supreme Giver and that *their first responsibility was to receive.*

For some reason, we generally hesitate to say and to stress that as Christians, our first responsibility is to receive. Perhaps we are reluctant to do so because it sounds selfish to say that our first act is to take. We had rather emphasize the duties of going, doing, and giving. Perhaps the reason that we sometimes are so sporadic in our going, so erratic in our doing, and so spasmodic in our giving of ourselves or what we have is that we have not first paused to receive.

We talk a great deal about Jesus' giving himself, and well we should. This was the outstanding mark of his life. But he also knew the value of receiving; he knew how to take from the hands of God and people. You will note that before his going, doing, or giving came his receiving strength, grace, and courage from his Father. In Jesus' Model Prayer in Matthew 6:11, one petition is phrased: "Give us this day our daily bread." No doubt, he used the word "give" in his conversations with the Father. Like small children who want what the parent is prepared to give, we are taught from the life of Christ to raise empty, open hands to God.

And Jesus knew how to take what sincere, grateful people offered to him. Recall the incident of the woman and her treasured ointment. She poured the costly ointment on Jesus as an act of love and gratitude. When some who were present criticized her for what they termed waste, Jesus sternly ordered that the woman be let alone. She had wanted to give what she could; his receiving what she offered was her satisfaction and fulfillment.

We come to a place and an hour of worship to acknowledge that somewhere in the past, we have received from God. We held out our empty hands as it were, for *forgiveness*. It was extended, and we took it gratefully. We asked for a *love* that would take us just as we were, that would not let us go, and that never would let us down. It was offered, and we took it. We lifted empty hands for *grace* which was strengthened and sustained. God gave, and we received in awed surprise that he would give so liberally.

We come in the experience of the supper to ask again, to receive from God, to acknowledge that every day is a day in which we go on receiving from God's wealth. As a song expresses so well, we come to lift up empty cups and ask that the Lord fill them. We ask that he fill them with mercy and love, with graciousness that we can share.

But as a fellowship celebrating Christ's presence, *we come to offer to each other and to receive from one another.* I think it is significant and suggestive that we pass the bread and juice to each other during the Lord's Supper. Christ is the ultimate source of what we receive: life and the necessary things of life. We take from him—to offer to each other. We offer, and we receive: friendship, loyalty, love, and support. If we are not willing to offer such to the fellow members of Christ's company, and if we are not willing to receive these when offered by our fellows, then I think that we do well to exclude ourselves from the supper. For I am convinced that this is at least part of what Paul meant by eating and drinking unworthily. In a context in which the Lord gave so much and those with him received a great deal, how can his people now be unwilling to offer and to take love, understanding, and forgiveness?

Our participation in this given meal is open acknowledgment that we have received, and continue to receive, from Christ. And it is a declaration that we engage in the interchange of offering and receiving from one another as his church.

19

A Time for Self-Examination

1 Corinthians 11:23-28

Introspection, the effort to take an objective look at ourselves, is extremely difficult for many of us to do. We have difficulty facing honestly and courageously what we find in the part of our lives that is hidden from those around us. For self-examination calls on us to deal with the undesirable which we know to be within us. Perhaps this is part of the reason we don't do more of it; maybe this is why many of us do not like silence and are afraid to be alone.

But self-examination is a vital part of the experience of participating in the Lord's Supper. As a fellowship, we come to share in this significant act of worship. We meet as Christ's followers to keep a form of worship that he instituted for us. But in a real sense, the supper places us alone in Christ's presence. When we are waiting to receive the bit of bread or the cup, while we hold them, or after we have partaken, we experience—or we should know—moments when our thoughts reach inward to the hidden places of our lives.

In these moments of reverent looking, we first must examine our relationship to Christ. Is it one in which we truly see ourselves as servants and see him as Lord? What is the degree of our commitment? Are we engaged in offering the best of which we are capable to Christ, or do we seek to give enough to maintain the comfortable feeling of self-satisfaction? In these moments, we need to reflect on Christ's self-giving on our behalf. He gave himself without reservation that we might be redeemed, that we might receive eternal life. And we must ask ourselves: what have

71

we done for him? what have we given to him?

Our relationship to Christ is strengthened and given added depth through our deliberate cultivation of the friendship that we share with him. Moments of sharing and listening, times of response to definite urgings and times of waiting, a serious study of Christ's life and a determined adopting of his spirit—all these go into our relationship with Christ. And in these moments, we reflect on that relationship, that friendship.

Second, we have an opportunity to reflect seriously on our relationship to Christ's church. In these moments, we are recreating the context in which Christ gave himself that people might experience redemption and become part of a redemptive community. He not only died on behalf of individuals but he also died for his movement of grace, the company of the called. As Paul wrote in Ephesians 5:25, "Christ also loved the church, and gave himself for it." Jesus spent much of his public ministry preparing his disciples to carry on his work; he died for his movement; he promised his presence; and he gave the redeemed community tremendous resources of power. How much have we given to and through the redeemed company? Is it just another social, fraternal organization to us? A religious club? A boring duty? Or is it the body of Christ, his organized, redemptive thrust in his world?

How we look at the church determines how much of ourselves we will give to it. If it is another one of people's grand schemes, based on Madison Avenue techniques, subtle propaganda, and calculating shrewdness and showmanship, then we can take it or leave it. But if it is God's family at work, if it is Christ's company obeying his directives, responding to his presence, and bent solely on doing his work, then we cannot take it or leave it. Not if we are truly Christian. The church becomes a priority with us, a must, a prized privilege. And, in these moments of reverent worship, we reflect on our relationship to the church as Christ's working crew in our world.

Third, we reflect on our relationship to each other as

individual Christians. How open are we to accept and to attempt to understand? How deeply do we care? How slow are we to judge and to condemn, and how swift to forgive? A church must be a group of people related to each other, people who realize that the cord which binds them together is the cord of grace, the chain of peace, the bond of love. We are people with a great deal in common; we are children of God, loved equally by him.

I never had any brothers and/or sisters; and, to my mind, whether this was an advantage or a disadvantage still is debatable. But I try to remind myself now that I have many brothers and sisters within God's family and that my opinions of them must be overshadowed by the fact that we call on the same Father. We are related, and therefore we must work together for the glory of our Father. In this worship experience, we have an opportunity to reflect on the strong ties among us.

For most of us, if not for all of us, reflection will lead to repentance. For in our relationships to Christ, his church, and individuals, some things need to be forgiven. We have done or said some things of which we are not proud, and we need a new starting place. Serious reflection on the things that really matter usually culminates in our asking that grace be granted for glaring failures.

Repentance, then, can lead to resolve—a determination that, by God's grace, our lives will be characterized by growth. We will be better people; our lives will be more productive and loving. It is always a resolve which says to Christ: "With your help, I will be more."

And so, the supper can be a time of reflection out of which come repentance and resolve. May it be so for us.

20

The Common and the Sacred

Mark 14:22-25

The Lord's Supper remains one of two significant acts of worship which Jesus instructed his followers to preserve. Through the centuries, the church has been careful to include the meal and baptism in its activities. No doubt, the early church observed the Lord's Supper far more frequently than we do. Other religious groups in our day participate in the supper much more often than Baptists generally do. If some have run the risk of reducing it to mere ritual, we well may have permitted this meal to become unimportant and practically meaningless.

The form of the meal has changed. On the night in which Jesus instituted the meal, he and his disciples had observed the Jewish Passover; they had eaten a full meal. After this meal, Jesus took a loaf of bread and a cup of the fruit of the vine and created an act of worship. Most likely, in the early church, the Lord's Supper was a full meal. Paul's words in 1 Corinthians 11, written in an effort to correct a distortion of the supper, imply as much. We come, receive a small piece of bread and a small cup of juice, and wonder what meaning such an act has.

Each time we participate in the Lord's Supper, we should endeavor to explore at least part of its meaning and significance for us. We constantly must attempt to understand the meal's depths. For I feel deeply that we need to be informed as well as reminded. We need to understand that the supper is, or should be, an act of deep worship by which we celebrate periodically our deliverance from personal bondage—a deliverance made possible by the One who gave us this meal. We need to employ the supper as a means of expressing our thanks to God. We need to be reminded of the essential unity of Christ's fellowship and of our participation in that unity. That we be impressed with the privilege given to us to enter a covenant relationship with One who gives life is crucial. And that we make this supper more than empty motion is imperative. We must allow it to be a creative experience in our pilgrimage as Christians.

This shared meal can be a dramatic reminder of the wholeness of our living as Christ's followers. Our lives are all of a single piece, though we often compartmentalize and fragment them. What the supper can do, if we permit, is to identify what we call the sacred with the common, the holy with the secular.

Interpreters often have pointed out that Jesus nowhere displayed his genius more dramatically than in his choice of a vehicle for a magnificent object lesson: a meal shared by his people. Further, he expressed his genius in his choice of two elements—bread and the fruit of the vine—to convey an ever-dynamic message. For these two were the most common elements in meals in that day.

Bread and the fruit of the vine were more than appropriate symbols of the context of agony in which the memorial meal was begun. Bread was made from wheat which grew as a result of a seed's being buried in the earth and dying. The fruit of the vine was made from grapes plucked from a vine and pressed in a stone vat. From the time of the first Lord's Supper, these two elements would convey the truth that real life for individuals comes as a result of Christ's death.

But something else is here, and it almost defies our attempts to define it clearly and neatly. Here, in the most sacred of worship experiences, are elements of the most common nature, materials that we take for granted. But we really should have expected it, for Jesus always identified with, and made use of, the common elements of life. His teachings were driven home to his hearers' minds by the use of the common things of life: birds, flowers, seeds, dough—and people. He used the common things to talk about himself: bread, water, light, and the vine. He identified with the joys and sorrows of common people.

Jesus never despised the common, material elements that make up such a large part of life. He saw nothing at all wrong with a person's asking God for the bread necessary to sustain life. He enjoyed life to the full, and he never was a hyperreligious wet blanket on others' celebrations.

One of the amazing things about Jesus is that he saw life as a whole; all of life was one vast field in which the Father worked. God was no more present in the Temple or synagogue than in a meal shared with people called sinners, by the seaside, on a mountain, or in the home of friends.

The bread and juice that we take remind us that God is active in every aspect of our living. God is present in our efforts to earn a living. The account in Genesis records that people's work took on the dimensions of toil because of revolt against God. By the sweat of their faces, Adam and those who came after him would obtain bread. And the use of bread in the Last Supper indicates that God has not abandoned people in their toil, but he is cognizant of and present in people's work.

The presence of the two common elements of bread and juice indicates that God is concerned with our celebrations as well as with our sorrows. These elements symbolize the truth that God is concerned with the family, education, business, and profession—all of those things that go to make up our lives. Jesus never consigned God to a restricted area of life marked "religion." And neither can we. To participate in his supper is to celebrate all of life. It is to celebrate God's concern with all of life and his activity in the whole of our experience.

In a real sense, every loaf and every cup become daily reminders of God's presence and activity in life. Every meal becomes an ordinance, a communion. For I am convinced that with God, the common or secular is sacred. What concerns people concerns the God who loves each of his creatures. The Lord's Supper conveys the truth that far from being removed from the elements of our living, God is present with us in each experience and at every moment.

21

Together, at the Lord's Table

1 Corinthians 11:23-28; 1 Corinthians 10:16-17

In 1 Corinthians, Paul dealt with a problem concerning the correct manner of participating in the Lord's Supper. But he also addressed a larger, overall problem in the Corinthian church, the problem of disunity and lack of harmony. Certain elements were present in the church that made the supper a hollow mockery and which caused a rending of the fabric of Christ's church.

In 1 Corinthians 10:16-17; 11:23-28, Paul wrote to a fragmented church. In his words, by implication, he stressed that people had to come to the Lord's table in a spirit of oneness and harmony. They had to come to the Lord's table *together* as one coordinated body directed by one Lord.

Paul's words maintain their relevance for our time. As we participate in this act, out of obedience to Christ, we do much more than review past history through a set of prescribed gestures. We do more than go through empty motions which mean little and do nothing. This suggestive experience can move us toward a new spirit of oneness if we understand the supper's significance and implications and if we allow what we do to have its proper impact on our lives.

Jesus ate the Jewish Passover meal with his disciples. Then, he originated his own meal. This might be called the new Passover for the new Israel. But what Christ inaugurated is an experience distinctive and unique to his church, the reconstituted people of God. Among other things, he meant his meal to be a sign of fellowship.

When we come to the Lord's table, we must realize that it is *his* table and not ours. The supper must be eaten in accord with his character and attitude, his spirit. Also, we are reminded that the church in which the experience of the supper is shared is *his* body; as members, we are *his* people. We share in something that he has made possible, something he has given to us.

Each time the church gathers to participate in the Lord's Supper, each member should be reminded of the essential oneness of Christ's people. Strength and effectiveness are derived from numbers only when fellowship and cooperation exist among the people. Here is one experience—the Lord's Supper—that is to be shared in unity if it is to be effective, productive. It can be meaningful only in fellowship.

In the supper itself and in the elements that are used, we can see promptings to unity among Christ's people. It is a stroke of Christ's genius that he used a meal as the basis of a continuing act of remembrance, commitment, and spiritual stimulation. The highest expression of friendship and shared goodwill in Christ's day was joint participation in a meal. Eating together was the strongest and most open display of fellowship. Quite possibly, Jesus meant his meal to stand as continuing and unmistakable evidence of the unity between him and his people. In the Fourth Gospel, John recorded for us Jesus' "high priestly prayer" in the context of Jesus' being betrayed and arrested. In this prayer recorded in John 17, Jesus expressed clearly his desire to be identified with his followers, his willingness to fellowship with them. The phrase "I in them" (vv. 23,26) was part of his prayer.

But in his prayer, Jesus also expressed another desire for his people: "That they all may be one; as thou, Father, art in me, and I in thee, that they also may be one in us" (v. 21). He went on to ask that his followers "be made perfect in one" (v. 23). Jesus wanted fellowship with every person, and he wanted fellowship between those who were his. These still are his desires. If this double unity, unity with him and with each other, was and is of such vital concern to him, then should it not be our concern as well?

In partaking of the Lord's Supper, we give evidence of our relationship to our Lord, and we express a relationship of sharing with one another. This is at least part of what our participation should mean.

Jesus took one loaf, broke it, and gave it to his disciples. Whether intentionally or not, this act stresses the wholeness of the body of Christ, his church, the fellowship which bears his name and experiences his presence. The emphasis is not that the body is fragmented, but that all believers partake of one fellowship. Paul made this clear in 1 Corinthians 10:16-17: "The cup of blessing which we bless, is it not the communion of the blood of Christ? The bread which we break, is it not the communion of the body of Christ? For we being many are one bread, and one body: for we are all partakers of that one bread." In the Gospel of John, Jesus declared that he is "the bread of life" (6:35).

In the same way, the cup emphasizes the unity of Christ's people. All the disciples at the first supper drank from one cup. The statement, "Drink ye all of it," in Matthew 26:27 means: all of you drink of it. This cup symbolized the institution of a new covenant authored by Jesus. All who become part of his covenant people share a common experience: they accept Jesus' life given for them. Christ's people are bound together by the grace which motivated him to give his life for us.

William Barclay expressed a stimulating, thought-provoking idea concerning eating and drinking unworthily at the Lord's table. He wrote that Paul's words may mean the person who eats and drinks unworthily is the one who never has realized that the church is Christ's body. Such an individual is, for some reason, not related to some other Christians in the church. Every person whose heart holds hatred, bitterness, or contempt against other people eats and drinks unworthily if, with that spirit, he or she comes to the Lord's table.

When we come to participate in the Lord's Supper, we are confronted with great truths: we serve one Lord; we are members of a common covenant; we share the same experience of grace; we share a common faith; we abide in the same Father's love; we share the same calling; we have received the same quality of life. In the light of these shared gifts of God, all our petty differences pale into insignificance. Together, we serve one Master, and we share the task of expressing his message of life to people around us—with one voice.

We approach the Lord's table—together.

22

Sharing His Cup

1 Corinthians 11:25

One of the most impressive Lord's Supper celebrations in which I have had the privilege of participating took place a number of years ago. What made the event so memorable and moving was the meditation presented by the pastor prior to the serving of the elements. Some years before, during a tour of Europe, he had found a beautiful silver goblet in one of the many shops through which he and his wife had browsed. He had been attracted by the goblet's beauty. He also had thought that something like that vessel had been used during the first Lord's Supper. So he had bought it; and it had remained one of his most treasured possessions. Now, he used it as a visible symbol to assist in worship. He held it in his hand as he talked about Jesus' sacrificing himself, pouring out his life, and the resulting redemption made available to all those who would receive it. During Jesus' brief ministry, he referred to a cup which was his alone to drink; and he drank it to the dregs. In the context of his meal, Jesus spoke of and offered a cup which his followers could share.

We are told that in usual practice, each participant had his own cup in the celebration of the Passover. In all the accounts of the institution of the Lord's Supper, the record reads that Jesus took his cup and passed it to his disciples with the charge that they all drink from it. In addition, he spoke of a covenant relationship established through his approaching death. A new relationship to God—a relationship based on grace—now was being made possible. In this new relationship, Christ's followers would be unified; they would share on the deepest possible level the gift of salvation and the demand of ministry.

Perhaps we are fortunate that the cup Jesus used on the night centuries ago has not survived the years. For people probably would have made the "Holy Grail" an object of worship and ascribed magical powers to it. Then, perhaps, the symbolism of the cup might not have called us to a sharing of Christ's kind of selfless service. I have come to feel that the cup Christ used symbolizes his total self-giving ministry in his life and death and that to drink from the cup is to express a willingness to serve, even at personal cost.

At least two disciples at that first supper must have reflected on the cup and Jesus' words concerning his life that he was about to give. I like to think that suddenly, their minds went back to an earlier incident in which they were involved and to words that Jesus had said then about his cup. Mark 10:35 records that James and John came to Jesus with a request; Matthew wrote (20:20) that a mother's ambitions for her sons created the situation. The request was that Jesus grant the two men a favor: when Jesus established his kingdom, let them occupy the places of honor; let them be seated by his side, one on the right and one on the left. Jesus replied that they did not know what they were asking. Note the exchange in Mark 10:38-39: "Can ye drink of the cup that I drink of? and be baptized with the baptism that I am baptized with?" he asked them. And the two had replied: "We can." Jesus answered: "Ye shall indeed drink of the cup that I drink of." For him, that cup contained ministry to people, suffering, sacrifice, and laying life on the line. James and John waited there in the upper room for the cup to be passed to them. They remembered. And they must have realized that Christ's cup is not to be taken lightly.

The use of the cup as dramatic symbolism was not new to any of those in the upper room. The writer of Psalm 23 had used it for God's generous provision for life: "My cup runneth over" (v. 5). The author of Psalm 75 had used the cup to sing about the bitter portion falling to the wicked. In Psalm 116, the writer had indicated that he would take the "cup of salvation" that God extended to him (v. 13). Isaiah 51:17 describes the consequences of evil as the cup of God's fury.

Jesus had taken the symbolism of the cup and had used it to impress on his disciples the kind of consistent service they were to offer in his spirit: Whosoever gives "a cup of cold water" (Matt. 10:42) in the spirit of discipleship will receive reward. On one occasion, he turned the statement around: those who offer Christ's servants "a cup of water" (Mark 9:41) will realize benefit. The cup forever has been made the symbol of the compassionate giving of what one has to another who needs it.

In addition to the incident involving James and John, on at least two other occasions Jesus used the cup to refer to his self-giving. In his remarkable prayer in Gethsemane, he said: "Abba, Father, all things are possible unto thee; take away this cup from me" (Mark 14:36). The "cup" symbolized the approaching agony of ultimate self-giving. In John 18:11, in response to Peter's attempt to defend him by force, Jesus asked: "The cup which my Father hath given me, shall I not drink it?"

And so, in the Lord's Supper celebration, we are offered Jesus' cup. And we are reminded of his request that all his followers drink of it. Our drinking is done in an awareness of privilege: the privilege of being part of a covenant community, of being in vital relationship to the Lord of life and to each other. But we also must have an awareness of demand. His cup is one of service, of self-giving in love. To drink of his cup means that we go out to be redemptive in our kind of world. We can share Christ's cup only at his invitation, with his encouragement, and in his strength. "Are you able to drink of my cup," he continues to ask us. And our answer must be: "not in our own strength, Lord, but only by your grace."

23

More than Mechanics

Mark 14:22-25

In the early days of the Christian movement, most of those outside the company of Christ did not understand the strange rite that Christians performed so frequently at meals. In fact, one of the charges brought against early Christians under fire was that of cannibalism; after all, did they not meet secretly and eat somebody's flesh and drink his blood? The Lord's Supper must have been a perplexing ceremony to those on the outside looking in.

It still must be. I am quite certain that for those outside the Christian fellowship who stop to observe what we do is strange and archaic, a left-over from a bygone age, a relic that has outlived its time and meaning. After all, many—and perhaps a majority—of those *within* the Christian community seldom if ever have paused to reflect at any length on the supper's meaning and far-reaching implications. If asked for an explanation of what we do and why we do it, many Christians would be hard pressed. They would have to struggle to get beyond the rather lame response that we do what Jesus did on the night of his arrest because he commanded that we repeat the movements in remembrance of him. What does this meal mean to me, here and now, in the ongoing flow of my living? What implications for serious meditation does it have for me today?

The implications are too many to be explored in a brief message. But one that I feel is worth consideration is found where we might least expect it—in the mechanics of what we do. Other implications are there, to be sure—in the bread, in the fruit of the vine, in the prayers of thanks, in the one cup and the one

85

loaf, and in the singing together before leaving. But even in the motions through which we go, most without thinking, is material for serious reflection.

I like the way Mark phrased his account of the institution of the Lord's Supper. A free rendering of what Mark wrote is: "and as they were eating, having taken bread, having blessed it, he broke and *gave* to them. . . . And having taken a cup, having given thanks, he *gave* to them." I get the feeling that here Mark was emphasizing what was so characteristic of Jesus throughout his ministry—his readiness to give.

In a previous Lord's Supper meditation, the accent was placed on the implication in what we do of our receiving from Christ and from one another in the fellowship that we experience in Christ. The other side of this particular coin is the implication of *giving,* Christ's and ours.

Jesus had given so much of his life's energies already. He had given out of his accumulated wisdom, out of his developed depth of spiritual insight, out of his amazing ability to make people whole, out of his supportive empathy for people of all kinds and of varying needs. He would go beyond this sacrificial giving of himself to make the supreme gift of life; he would move through the valley of deepest darkness for the redemption of those who were wrong. And still he would not be done with giving himself. He would give his continued presence in support, sharing, and supplying strength for each day's demands.

In the inauguration of his meal, Jesus gave the bread and the cup to his disciples as they reclined at the table. Probably, each man gave these in turn to the one next to him. In our participation, we give the bread and the cups to those next to us on the pews. In this act, this part of the meal's mechanics, whether we are aware of it or not, we acknowledge that giving of ourselves lies at the heart of Christian discipleship. It is a demand placed on us by One who gave himself for us. It is something that we must work at doing.

Some people I have met along my way have caught hold of this concept. They must have. They gave so much to me without asking anything in return, which is fortunate for me, for I could not possibly repay them in kind. People who give always have impressed me: not primarily those who give things, though these often are expressions of an awesome generosity, but those who give what ultimately counts out of the depths of their lives. When the deep in me has called out to the depth that is God, not only has he answered but also people often have met me in love and concern.

I have come face-to-face with a marvelous and disturbing truth: the greatest and most needed gifts come out of life's depths—gifts on which no price can be placed and great acts of giving which cost the giver. The gifts from life's depths include friendship which is more than surface politeness or the offering of a hand in greeting or parting; understanding which works to place oneself in another's shoes or inside his or her skin; sympathetic support which goes far beyond words; love that allows another the comfort and relief of letting the real self show—"warts and all." These are not casual, cheap, commonplace gifts. This kind of giving represents sizable expenditures of the stuff of our lives. And at the same time, in the long run, this kind of giving is most rewarding.

In our celebration of the Lord's Supper, I am glad that each person can be involved in passing the elements, giving them to the neighbor in the pew. For that is an act highly symbolic, more than mechanics. It is expressive of a demand which we must be attempting to meet every day of our lives: the demand to give of ourselves.

24

Ritual or Renewal?

Luke 22:14-20

The most common, prevalent danger in frequent repetition of a procedure is that the procedure becomes routine. It becomes something that we do without thinking, something repeated by rote. It becomes familiar to the point that the person or persons who are involved consider it "old hat." This danger always is present in our reenactment of the Lord's Supper, and we must guard against it constantly. For *what was intended to be a vibrant means of renewal can be reduced to lifeless ritual.*

Most evangelical Christians have been, and are, staunchly anti-ritual. They do not care much for rigidly structured, formal rites of worship with repetition of written creeds. Generally, they avoid being liturgical or "high church." Yet, curiously, we have rituals which we never call by that name. Our *programs of worship* become rituals when we can run through them without thinking and when we resist change in them, no matter how constructive, because of attachment to the familiar. *Baptism* can, and too often does, become ritual when it is viewed as a matter of course without reverence and reflection on the part of candidates and congregation. *Ordination* can become ritual when people do not give proper thought to the seriousness and significance of what is being done. It becomes ritual when the laying on of hands becomes a curious relic of an ancient rite rather than an open acknowledgment of spiritual qualities which equip one for leadership. As much as we might be tempted to criticize other denominations for their rigid, formal systems of worship, we, too, have our rituals.

And the cold, hard fact is that the Lord's Supper can become mere ritual unless we take steps to protect this unique celebration that Jesus gave to his people. We reduce it to going through familiar steps which have no meaning when we do not allow the symbols used and the actions performed to be avenues of worship and renewal.

To look on the supper and our participation in it as unimportant—so insignificant that one feels if one is going to miss a period of collective worship, this is a good one to miss—is one thing. To me, that is serious and unfortunate misthinking, detrimental to the person and to the company of Christ. To make the supper a ritual by merely repeating motions rather than allowing it to be effective, productive worship is something else altogether—and just as serious.

The Lord's Supper can be one of our finest means of needed periodic renewal as Christ's people. It is deeply significant to me that many times, near the beginning of a new church year, we participate in the supper. Our celebration at this juncture speaks—or should speak—of our deep desire to experience spiritual renewal as individuals and as a church.

Celebrated at a time of new beginning, the start of a new calendar year or a new church year, the Lord's Supper can be *a means of renewing our relationships to Christ and to each other.* It may be that one prayer many of us may have to pray as we partake of the elements of the supper is the prayer David phrased so long ago in Psalm 51: "Restore unto me the joy of thy salvation" (v. 12). "Create in me a clean heart, O God; and renew a right spirit within me" (v. 10). We can put it into more familiar words: "I have drifted away from you; I have grown cold, closed, and careless. I have left you out of too many things, too many times. Let me experience the warmth and security of your presence again." Whatever the words are, serious meditation on Christ's suffering and self-sacrifice can lead to new openness to him.

And if we see ourselves as God's family gathered around his table, we might be impressed with an essential truth. If we can share in his meal together, the possibility is that we can live together in some degree of openness and in an extended goodwill that persists even when it is rejected. Renewed relationships to people can issue from the right celebration of the Lord's meal.

What we do in the Lord's Supper can be *a means of our renewing our gratitude*—for redemption made available at staggering cost; for Christ's presence here and in our individual lives, providing a continuing source of spiritual strength; for provision to meet daily needs of living; for the promise of our sharing in ultimate victory. That Christ's people ever could become ungrateful is almost incomprehensible, yet we do. A new look at the cross should renew our almost inexpressable appreciation for the life that we have been given.

And out of renewed relationships to Christ and to each other, and renewed gratitude for life with the dimension and quality of the eternal, can come *renewed involvement in Christ's church.* In a recreated context of Christ's suffering and death, we are reminded that he gave himself to redeem people through whom the good news of salvation by grace through faith can be expressed. The conditions then are met for a fresh, new dedication to the ministry of his church. For, in reality, the church is the extension of Christ's ministry, his self-giving service, to people. We are his body, the embodiment of his compassion, his love, and his strong and courageous conviction. By who we are and what we stand for, we embody his judgment on wrong by making sharp and clear the contrast between godliness and self-seeking.

Can you begin to imagine the mixed feelings of pride and humility with which the disciples and others in the early church celebrated the Lord's meal? To include pride and humility in one experience sounds paradoxical, I know. But I sometimes feel just a little something of what they must have felt. Open pride at being identified with the company of the Galilean Carpenter, being known as his person, and taking part in something distinctly his. Humility at the realization that I am unqualified for such inclusion apart from his gracious acceptance. Humility at the repeated realization of responsibility and demand which goes with being in his company.

The Lord's Supper—is it mere familiar ritual, or is it an instrument of renewal? What do we make it?

25

Strength for Struggle

Mark 14:22-26

I had read the accounts of the institution of the Lord's Supper countless times. I had taken part in the public reading of it; I had shared in responsive readings or had read aloud to congregations the earliest record written by Paul in 1 Corinthians or the earliest Gospel record in Mark. I had prepared a number of Lord's Supper meditations in an attempt to contribute to the building of a proper setting for this meaningful act of the church in remembrance of its Lord. But I had continued to miss an extremely graphic and significant detail of the supper in which Jesus and his disciples participated so long ago. And I had missed the implication of this detail for us in our participation in this meal. Like most active Christians, I had begun to understand something of the dramatic context of the supper, the implications of its being instituted at the time of the Jewish Passover. I had pondered the deep symbolism of the bread and the fruit of the vine. But for too long, I had stopped too soon in my reflections on the Lord's Supper.

Mark 14:26 states: "And when they had sung a hymn, they went out into the mount of Olives." Now, the singing of psalms was a normal part of the Passover observance. Interpreters have suggested that Jesus and his disciples sang Psalms 115—118. These psalms have to do with God's sovereignty and trustworthiness to help Israel, thanksgiving for deliverance from death, praise for God's mercy, and gratitude for God's salvation. Especially fitting for this occasion, when Jesus was facing betrayal, rejection, and death, was Psalm 118.

First of all, I was surprised to realize that Jesus sang with his disciples. George Buttrick wrote insightfully that we usually think of Jesus as being haggard with woe as he went to his cross. Certainly he did not welcome the cross; but here, as the shadow of this cruel means of execution fell across him, he could sing! With courage and resolve, he could express trust in God and gratitude for deliverance. And he could encourage a perplexed, confused band of men to sing with him—and to believe what they were singing.

I cannot begin to imagine what went on inside Jesus as he sang the words of Psalm 118:5-6: "I called upon the Lord in distress: the Lord answered me, and set me in a large place. The Lord is on my side; I will not fear: what can man do unto me?" A little later, in verse 14, the writer affirmed: "The Lord is my strength and song, and is become my salvation." Then, the psalmist expressed his confidence in verses 17-18: "I shall not die, but live, and declare the works of the Lord. The Lord hath chastened me sore: but he hath not given me over unto death." Included in this Psalm, in verse 22, are words which later came to mean much to the early Christians: "The stone which the builders refused is become the head stone of the corner." What significance these words would have to One who, in obedience to the Father, was about to give himself for people!

Jesus and his disciples were engaged in worship which fortified them for what would follow; from fellowship involving stirring psalms, they received strength for the struggle. This is what should occur in every worship period, especially when we enjoy the fellowship around the Lord's table.

Much of our worship—and even our participation in the Lord's Supper—can be mere form. The singing of the hymn at Passover was a part of what Jews usually did, and it may have started here in the upper room as adherence to usual form. But it became much more. Halford Luccock penetratingly observed that, as Jesus and the disciples shared in their nation's great heritage of faith, they discovered "a power arming their minds and hearts against whatever might be waiting for them." These men found an experience of renewal which they would need repeated periodically in the days and years ahead.

After Jesus and his disciples had sung a hymn, they went out. Halford Luccock has asked what is true of us. "Is it true that we do not 'go out' more effectively in the conflict with evil because we do not worship effectively enough? Is it true that after we have sung a hymn we all too often sit down instead of going out at all? The hymns we sing and the prayers we offer have to take deep inward hold if there is to be any projection outward."[1]

In a written prayer, a housewife shared her reflections on participation in the Lord's Supper. She confessed that she took Communion, eating the bit of unleavened bread and drinking the little cup of juice, knowing that she should be worshiping but not doing so. Later, in quiet moments, she communed with Christ. She stated her inability to understand all that the meal means, though she knew that she should have an awareness of newly-received forgiveness and a new dedication. And she meditated on the fact that Jesus and his disciples ate, drank, sang a hymn, and went out into the night. "What a way to face night, Lord! What a strength and a shield—to face whatever the night may hold for us with a joy, a triumphant joy in the heart, and a hymn of praise—a stirring, undergirding hymn of praise."[2]

Worship, especially when it takes the form of the Lord's Supper, is many things. But one thing it ought to be is *a gathering of strength to face the nights and days of our living*—strength from the Lord of the church who is present, and strength from each other. We need to gather strength for the challenges, crises, and opportunities that we will meet. We should meet, pray, read Scriptures, and sing. Then, after we have participated in the supper, we can go out with fresh power and incentive to engage the events of our lives. We can go out as those who share the victory in life won by the Christ whom we worship by participating in his meal.

NOTES

1. Luccock, *T.I.B.,* Vol. 7, p. 879.
2. Jo Carr and Imogene Sorley, *Too Busy Not to Pray* (Nashville, New York: Abingdon Press, 1966), p. 77.

26

Supper of Commitment

Mark 14:12-25

One of the fascinating things about the Lord's Supper to me is its many facets. A meal, instituted by Christ and given to his church to be enjoyed repeatedly, has become the vehicle for almost limitless meaning to those who participate in reverence, faith, and honest petition. Meditation on the meaning of the Lord's Supper brings fresh insight concerning its strong implications to the servant church of a servant Lord.

Christ's meal is a *supper of sharing,* displaying in one united act the solidarity of Christ's people. It is a meal which *activates memory* and causes us to review Christ's redemptive acts on our behalf. The supper is a means of *celebrating deliverance—*personal deliverance from wrong and self-centeredness. It is an act which *renews our covenant* relationship with our Lord. The meal is a corporate *giving of thanks* for full life. In its use of simple, common elements, the supper removes our distinction between *the common and the sacred.* And out of our participation as a body comes *strength for the continuing struggle* to be Christ's people in a society which needs him and what he continues to do and to say. I have been amazed at the variety of lessons and the depth of meaning to be found in the vivid scene and the creative words of the Lord's Supper.

The thought has occurred to me that among the many significant meanings to be gleaned from our participation in this meal is the truth that we share a supper of commitment. Because we are mortal, we have to review our commitments periodically to keep fresh our awareness of that to which we have pledged ourselves. This is true in various areas of our living: in marriage and family, friendships, vocations, community activities, and educational pursuits. If we are not careful and attentive, we forget or neglect to fulfill an original commitment.

One vital service which the Lord's Supper does for us is to keep before us the pledge that we made in a moment of sincere response to the living Christ and to allow us to renew that pledge. The supper is for those who are determined followers of Christ, and it will not allow us to forget the demands involved in such following.

If we participate in the Lord's Supper with understanding, we become aware that *we are renewing our commitment to Christ*. Commitment involves our total lives, our dedication of what we are and have without reservation. In the case of the Christian, this commitment is to the Person. I have been impressed with what people can accomplish when they are committed to a cause. I have seen serious, enthused people undertake projects which I honestly thought were beyond their reach. Yet, through their dedication translated into determined work, they reached their goal.

And the thought has impressed itself on me: Christianity is not a cause or merely a movement; it is a way of life in relationship to the Person. How much deeper and stronger should be commitment to this Person who gives full life than to anyone or anything else? Often, I have wondered what would happen in churches, families, and neighborhoods if commitment to Christ came before every other commitment. What if our pledge to him were honored first? My mind cannot grasp the creative change that would result or the quality of life which would be produced.

If we don't have the rich, full, personal relationships that we want or the depth of spirit in our churches which often is so conspicuous by its absence or a healthy atmosphere of community which helps to nurture life, the primary reason lies in our shallow or nonexistent commitment to Christ. The Lord's Supper is a vehicle for the reverent, serious renewal of the pledge of our lives to Christ.

The meal that we share also is a means of *recommitting ourselves to each other.* One puzzling observation I have made is that so few of us seem to understand that, when we commit life to Christ, *we also commit ourselves to the members of his company.* We present a strange picture to those around us, I am sure, when we pledge ourselves to Christ and keep each other at arm's length or farther.

Christ made clear to his disciples that one open to him also must be open to the other members of God's family. One of the most definite proofs of our being Christ's followers is our active care for one another. In John 13:35, Jesus said: "By this shall all men know that ye are my disciples, if ye have love one to another." And to love in the sense that Christ meant without committing ourselves to each other's highest good is impossible.

One early writer, recording information about the earliest Christians, wrote that what impressed those who viewed the Christians in action was their care for each other. The early Christians sincerely loved one another, and they showed it. The supper should cause us to review our commitment to each other in a love that runs the risk of being rejected, a determined goodwill that is not easily discouraged.

Last, this shared meal reminds us that our commitment to Christ and to the members of his company is *a commitment to serve.* We stay ready to function in whatever capacity our abilities allow for the advancement of Christ's work. We do this in the knowledge that Jesus adopted the servant role and he called his followers servants. In his servant role, he was Master and Lord to those who made him so. If Jesus served people, how much more should his followers do so? For the servant is not better than his Master. We accept the benefits Christ provides. Therefore we should seek to share these benefits with others.

27

The Cost of Winning

Mark 14:22-24

I ran across the idea of the cost of winning in a little book written by J. B. Phillips dealing with the Lord's Supper. The title of the book is *Appointment with God: Some Thoughts on Holy Communion.* Phillips wrote:

> If the truth be told, men are often willing to put their trust in a god who in the end must be triumphant, simply because they want to be on the winning side; but they are not nearly so ready to bear any part of the cost of that winning. Yet the fellowship of the broken bread and the poured-out wine can mean no less than that.[1]

We come to the moments of the Lord's Supper to participate in celebration. We come to affirm victory, triumph, conquest. From our privileged vantage point on this side of the resurrection, we can celebrate *the cross* as Jesus' coronation. A cruel stake became the Redeemer's throne. We are able to understand clearly how Jesus could speak of the cross as the means of his being glorified. We affirm together that an execution has become a means of salvation and an eternal triumph because of God's power to salvage good out of evil.

We gather at the Lord's table to celebrate *anticipated victory,* for we restate our absolute conviction of Christ's triumphant return, the consummation of history in God's good time. We say that a time will come when the curtain will fall on the scene of which we now are part, when time runs out into eternity suddenly and without warning. Then, indeed, every eye will see him, every knee will bow, and every tongue will confess that God is sovereign. We come to reaffirm that it will happen—not when the world finally becomes wicked enough or when crises become so severe that only divine intervention can solve them, but when God decides that quite literally, time is up.

But we also come to celebrate a third kind of victory: *conquest in the process of life.* We come as those trusting totally the One who once said to his followers: "In the world ye shall have tribulation: but be of good cheer; I have overcome the world" (John 16:33). Paul wrote: "We are more than conquerors through him that loved us," (Rom. 8:37). Because of our response to God-in-Christ, ultimately we will share in triumph; more than that, we can be enabled to live triumphantly *now.* Some of us do celebrate victorious living in these moments of worship: a winning over problems, habits, temptations, or self through faith in the present Christ. Some of us, if not all of us, no doubt come to admit losing some battles but still are intent confidently on winning the war.

But notice carefully: *cost is involved in winning.* No one ever has won in war, political campaign, athletic contest, or struggle to live on the highest moral level without tremendous cost. High cost was involved for Jesus. In every facet of his life and ministry, he had a price to pay for his winning in the effort to effect redemption. The cost for him was a lifetime of absolute obedience; part of the cost to him was a faith-to-follow exercised each day. He paid an awesome price in terms of sharing himself. Mark's Gospel has a scene which, to me, indicates that Jesus' work of making people whole cost him. Jairus, a ruler of the synagogue, came and asked Jesus to go to his home and restore his seriously ill daughter to health. On the way, a woman troubled with a severe, long-term hemorrhage touched the fringe of Jesus' robe in a search for healing. Jesus stopped to ask who had touched him; for, as Mark recorded, Jesus knew that virtue had gone out of him. Jesus' effort "took something out of him" when he helped suffering, sinful people. Finally, of course, the cost for him in terms of physical, mental, and emotional pain and a poured-out life was staggering. But he won. The verdict of history and eternity always will be clear: he won.

Three haunting verses in the Book of Hebrews reflect something of the cost of winning to Jesus. In 5:7-9, the author of Hebrews wrote of Jesus:

> Who in the days of his flesh, when he had offered up prayers and supplications with strong crying and tears unto him that was able to save him from death, and was heard in that he feared; Though he were a Son, yet learned he obedience by the things which he suffered; And being made perfect, he became the author of eternal salvation unto all them that obey him.

Jesus paid an awesome price for victory.

Cost is involved for us in our being winners. Victory in living costs our being open to God's leading, even when he leads where we prefer not to go. Winning costs in our bearing Christ's cross: giving in his spirit when no prospect of return exists—and not even an expression of thanks. It costs in the day-by-day work of ministry to people when results are hard to see or nonexistent. Winning costs in swallowing pride, taking the blows, and going the second mile when we are bone weary from the first mile.

Sharing in winning costs in the long and painful struggle to find in ourselves that which God can use, and then to give it to his use. Part of what being a Christian means—and a significant part—is finding our particular gifts and developing them as highly as possible.

When we come to share in this significant act so filled with meaning for Christ's followers—when we eat unleavened bread and drink a small container of juice—we celebrate victory and acknowledge the cost of conquering. And we demonstrate our willingness to share in that cost. We are not merely spectators of something that Christ has done; we are participants in what he *is doing* in life.

NOTE
1. J. B. Phillips, *Appointment with God: Some Thoughts on Holy Communion* (London: The Epworth Press, 1954), p. 38.

28

Is It I?

Mark 14:18-19

Several years ago, as I began to think about a meditation around which my congregation and I could center some serious thinking in our participation in the Lord's Supper, I read again the accounts of the meal in the three Gospels and in 1 Corinthians. In a number of previous meditations, I had tried to single out various facets of the supper. I attempted to present these as reminders, challenges, and demands that were needed greatly in our personal pilgrimages and in our life together. As I read, I was struck again by some interesting and suggestive factors in the context of the supper, in words and acts which both immediately preceded and followed the meal. The more I probed, the more I found to apply, first of all to myself, and then to the participants.

Passover was approaching. The disciples asked Jesus where he would like to celebrate the feast so that they could make preparations. Jesus already had arranged for a place that offered the privacy he desired for these final, crucial hours alone with his men. The disciples followed his instructions and readied the meal. In the evening, Jesus gathered with his men in the upper room. As they were eating, Jesus surprised and stunned them by saying: "Verily I say unto you, One of you which eateth with me shall betray me" (Mark 14:18). I can imagine that for one long, silent moment, everything stopped. Hands with food halfway to mouths paused; mouths savoring morsels froze in mid-chew; conversations ceased. All eyes were on Jesus. Then the disciples looked at one another. One by one, they began to ask Jesus: "Is it I?" (v. 19).

Some have looked at this question of the disciples and have

seen it as an attempt to deny guilt and shift suspicion to the rest. The question literally is: "Not I?" We would say, "It is not I, is it?" "Surely not I?" The question may have been a way of protesting innocence. But as I read the stunned question, something else comes through to me. I get the feeling that eleven of the disciples who asked the question somehow felt themselves capable of betrayal and asked Jesus for his insight. Rather than being an attempt at evasion and denial, I see their asking as spontaneous honesty: "I might be the one even though I am not conscious of it."

The question remains live, pertinent for us. I am convinced that deep within the recesses of our souls, you and I—in these moments of keeping an ordinance—need to ask ourselves the question: Is it I?

In all likelihood, we are reluctant to do it—to place ourselves at the table with Jesus to dip in the dish with him and to hear his words concerning betrayal. But in a real sense, like it or not, if we profess to be his people, we sit and eat with him, our Companion—"the Man who eats with us"—and we hear his words.

But do we hear his words? They are there, but we feel much more comfortable when we assign them to an upper room that belonged to a Jerusalem of nearly twenty centuries ago, addressed to Judas. As Halford Luccock pointed out, betrayal is a harsh word; traitor is a despised title. Because of Judas' betrayal of Jesus, his name has become a repulsive word. Because of his act, Benedict Arnold has become the epitome of disgraceful treachery. We are not quick to claim such company.

Luccock was right: if we see betrayal as overt, once-for-all renunciation of loyalty, allegiance, then few if any of us will see ourselves as capable of a denial of Christ as our Lord. We are not likely to stand up and repudiate our being Christians; we are not likely to denounce our membership in the community of the redeemed. But betrayal in the Christian life usually does not come that way; it presents itself in any number of subtle choices which progressively lead us over the edge.

I deny Christ when I let my devotion grow cold. So do you. When we go on our ways, unaware that our faith has grown shallow, that our interest has waned, that our love has weakened, we are living denials of Christ. When we see no need of renewal, and when experiencing new vitality in our relationship with our Lord does not concern us, we betray him.

When my interests, my goals, and my desires take precedence and push the desires and purposes of Christ to a secondary position, I betray him. I proclaim him Lord and attempt to make him serve my purposes; I seek his sanction for my chosen ends instead of asking for direction. The most subtle form of betrayal is to claim to be a Christian and to fail to allow Christ to be *the* determining force in life.

When we allow the context of our living to determine our view of and allegiance to Christ, we betray him.[1] Paul wrote: "Be not conformed to this world: but be ye transformed by the renewing of your mind" (Rom. 12:2). If we allow ourselves to be influenced by an environment in which Jesus is disregarded, ignored, or merely patronized, instead of influencing that environment with the vitality of his love and grace, then we betray him.

When we talk about Jesus' principles for living and engage in no serious struggle to live by them, we betray him. When we nod approval to self-giving, mercy, brotherhood, and compassion, and show little or no attempt to make them more than words or ideas, we deny the One who goes on saying that these are important expressions of redeemed life.

I wonder if one of the questions that you and I just might need to ask ourselves in these moments—and to answer honestly—is one asked by troubled disciples in an upper room: "Lord, is it I?"

NOTE
1. Luccock, *T.I.B.,* Vol. 7, p. 876.

29

Challenge to Dependability

Luke 22:28

I suppose that I would have gone on missing it had I not read the printed wisdom of one of the most remarkable ministers I know anything about. Over thirty years ago, this individual chose a passage in Luke as the basis for thoughts on the Lord's Supper, thoughts intended to encourage followers of Christ in an extremely difficult stretch of the twentieth century. I had read the account in Luke many times; I had prepared numerous meditations for participation in the supper. But I had missed the full impact of one dramatic statement Jesus made to his disciples. Now when I read the passage, the sentence leaps out at me with all of its implications for me as a twentieth-century disciple—and for all of Christ's followers in a troubled time.

Luke gave a somewhat extended account of the institution of the Lord's Supper. Just as Mark before him, he gave details of a meal that Jesus arranged during the Jewish Passover celebration. Luke recorded Jesus' careful preparations for a private room in which he and his disciples could share a meal. He presented the stark drama of Jesus' actions as the group reclined at the table: giving the cup with suggestive words about its symbolic meaning; distributing the bread. And the dark note Jesus sounded about one who would betray him lingered in the room.

Then Luke alone recorded that, in the upper room setting, the disciples began to argue about who was number one in the group. See the scene, hear the words, feel the drama in your imagination. Time was running out in a hurry for Jesus. Added to the pressure of impending crisis was the imperative need to say some things to his disciples that would make a lasting impression on their minds—words that would draw their attention to their great responsibility. He wanted to give words that would assure, inspire, and instruct. He was thinking about the awesome task of redeeming people and about the terrible specter of death. His disciples were quibbling about rank in his company; they were concerned with settling the issue of greatness. Then, during a momentary lull in the claims and counterclaims of eminence, Jesus said softly: "Ye are they which have continued with me in my temptations" (22:28). I can imagine that all at once, things got quiet as those words began to sink in. The words would stay with them, even when they desperately wished that they could forget. The fact that Luke preserved this statement of Jesus, even though he was the only one to do so, says that the early church could not forget what Jesus said following the meal with his disciples.

The disciples' immediate reaction must have been shame, embarrassment, and discomfort. Previously, Jesus had spoken of his self-giving, the awesome cost of life for individuals and for his church; they had fallen to quarreling about rank in his company. "Ye are they which have continued with me in my temptations," Jesus said. And gentle rebuke was present: "You did not learn this over-concern about greatness from me; rather, if you have paid attention, you have learned service from me."

Beyond this immediate reaction, the disciples must have remembered times when they had let Jesus down. James and John must have recalled the time when they had wanted to call down fire on some Samaritans who had refused to extend hospitality to Jesus and his men. The two brothers had been so slow to learn love for all people; they had added to Jesus' already heavy burden. Peter must have thought of the time he had confessed that Jesus was the Son of God and then immediately had disputed Jesus' statement that Jesus would suffer and die. Jesus had rebuked him sharply. Peter had intensified Jesus' anguish over the disciples' misunderstanding of him. The others could recall times when they had failed to support Jesus, to listen attentively, and to share his concern.

And later, after the crucifixion and resurrection, Jesus' men would remember how they had let him down—how three in the garden had failed to pray with him, how they all had deserted him, how confused and fearful and discouraged they had been before they knew that death had not conquered him. "You are the ones who stood by me in my trials," Jesus said in essence. And I can imagine that when they remembered his words, they bowed their heads in renewed repentance. Then they lifted their heads with a renewed determination to be the kind of people who were consistently responsive and faithful to the Lord who still was present with them.

But something else made Jesus' words unforgettable, something which would offer encouragement and strength for dark days, when work for Christ would be difficult and trying. Something like a note of gratitude must have been in Jesus' voice as he said softly: "Ye are they which have continued with me in my temptations." As Harry Emerson Fosdick pointed out, these men were not much for which to be grateful, and they probably knew it. But they remembered what Jesus said and felt a lift to their spirits. They were ordinary people. They had been wrong; they had failed; they had been weak. But Jesus had chosen them. And at the last, he had thanked them for staying with him, no matter if they had stumbled frequently. They must have remembered this with the right kind of pride, the kind of pride which produces a happiness at being part of something good and worthwhile. They must have felt the kind of pride which moved them to make greater effort, to be better persons, to go on trying somehow to earn the gratitude that had been expressed for effort that they knew to be less than the best.

If we can comprehend the awesome truth, Christ is present in our celebration. And he says to those of us who are his: "Ye are they which have continued with me in my temptations." And in a moment of flashing honesty, we remember our failures, our wrongs, our moments of weakness. We know that we are those who have offered less than our best, and some of us have allowed ourselves to become discouraged, lazy, indifferent, or satisfied. And yet, the Lord of the church says to us: "Ye are they. . . ." That should cause many of us repentant embarrassment—and yet, a gratitude at being included which will cause us to be determined people.

As we participate in the Lord's Supper and thereby recreate the context in which Jesus said something remarkable and surprising to his disciples, we need to ponder his words. They are spoken to us at this time, in this place. We are the ones on whom he is counting to continue with him in all the crucial tests confronting the church for which he gave himself. *Are* we the ones on whom he can continue to depend?

30

From the Supper—To What?

Mark 14:26

Most of us who have been Christians for any length of time are familiar with the procedure followed in the church's participation in the Lord's Supper. If the total worship period is built around the supper, usually included in the program of worship is a brief meditation centered on some aspect of the meal as recorded in the Gospels and in 1 Corinthians. Jesus' movements are repeated: the prayer of thanks for the loaf, the distribution of the fragments of bread, the eating in reverent meditation; the blessing of the juice, the passing of the cups, the drinking as an outward sign of being numbered in Christ's covenant community. Most of us know the steps—so well that sometimes they are done without thought, emptied of meaning.

But what happened *after* that first meal in the upper room? The meal that Jesus instituted was rich in implications for the church being formed by one who was on his way to giving himself to redeem responsive people. It was one of those high, creative moments intended to give the disciples motivation for living in future days, strength for labor, and courage for risk. So much material was present in this multifaceted meal for the disciples' reflection and absorption! They went from the upper room to Gethsemane; three of them went into the depths of the garden to be nearer to Jesus while he prayed. He asked that they watch with him. They went to sleep. Three times. When the mob led by Judas arrived at the garden, Mark recorded pointedly: "And they all forsook him, and fled" (Mark 14:50). Two of the disciples followed at a distance as the mob led Jesus away; one later denied knowing him. From an upper room of warm fellowship and creative teaching to a low of dullness, desertion, and denial—what a distance these men traveled in a short time! They later recovered and went on to keep the meal as a part of their life as the church. But what followed the first meal contains lessons for us.

What happens when we leave the Lord's Supper? Or any period of worship, for that matter? What follows that which is designed to be a high moment in the life of Christ's church? We can't be too harsh with the disciples; we can't use their failure to feel superior. We are a lot like they were—expressly human with strengths and weaknesses. For the most part, we differ little from them. We are no more sensitive, no more aware, no stronger, no more courageous. We share something with them: a tendency to leave lofty moments of worship in a format given by Jesus to continue life-as-usual, largely unchanged, unaffected by the unique.

Years ago, some preacher or teacher whose name and face now are beyond my power to recall made a point that I haven't forgotten. Often, after our highest moments of meaningful experiences, we are most vulnerable to temptation, susceptible to error, prone to letdown. Continuing experience tends to confirm the truth of that idea.

We can go from the supper to dullness in a time demanding alertness. We can leave to sleep peacefully in a critical span in our history. We can be "caught napping" in a world desperately in need of the salt and light of vibrant Christianity. More and more, in a predominately impersonal society, people are looking for those who can bring warmth to their coldness, light to their darkness, joy to their despair by the personal touch, attention to them and their hurts which expresses care. If we are alert, more opportunities than we can grasp are available to us to bring grace to bear on the hurts of the world. Preoccupation with a small circle of interest will dull awareness to a wider circle of potential service. Christian ministry demands alertness.

We can leave the supper to resume a casual attitude toward worship, personal spiritual growth, and service that constitutes a gradual moving away from Christ and his church. Disinterest, indifference, constitutes a withdrawal from Christ's demands to a safe distance instead of studied, determined involvement in his purpose. It means leaving Christ to bear the cross alone, while we go free from responsibility.

We can go from the supper to a practical denial of the confirmation theoretically made by our sharing in the meal. By taking the bread and drinking from the cup, we make our profession that we are Christ's people, called by his name, possessing his presence, doing his work. How is this confession expressed in other places, at other times—or is it evident at all? Our confession can be continued by the spirit with which we live, by the values we possess, and by the principles which shape our acts. The faith which lies at the center of our lives should be expressed and shared in crisis and in celebration and in our struggle to love as the One whom we claim as Lord has commanded us. Our denial is pragmatic when we live as though Christ really doesn't count, actually has no bearing on our living, has nothing vital to say to us. We confirm our profession when we allow him to speak and act through us.

From the supper—to what? To sleep, withdrawal, denial? Or to new awareness, loyalty, profession? Which is it for me, for you?